Betty Crocker

comfort
food

100 Recipes for the Way You Really Cook

BICENTENNIAL
1807
WILEY
2007
BICENTENNIAL

Wiley Publishing, Inc.

Library of Congress Cataloging-in-Publication Data:
Betty Crocker comfort food : 100 recipes for the way you really cook.
   p. cm.
Includes index.
ISBN 978-0-470-17350-3 (cloth)
1. Comfort food. I. Crocker, Betty. II. Title: Comfort food.
TX740.B516 2007
641.3--dc22

2007013681

General Mills

Directors, Book and Online Publishing:
Maggie Gilbert and Lynn Vettel

Manager, Cookbook Publishing: Lois Tlusty

Recipe Development and Testing:
Betty Crocker Kitchens

Photography and Food Styling: General Mills
Photography Studios and Image Library

Wiley Publishing, Inc.

Publisher: Natalie Chapman

Executive Editor: Anne Ficklen

Project Editor: Adam Kowit

Editor: Lauren Brown

Production Manager: Leslie Anglin

Cover Design: Suzanne Sunwoo

Art Director: Tai Blanche

Layout: Indianapolis Composition Services

Manufacturing Manager: Kevin Watt

Manufactured in China

10 9 8 7 6 5 4 3 2

Wiley Anniversary Logo: Richard J. Pacifico

Cover photo: Onion and Bacon Grilled Cheese Sandwiches (page 118)

Our Betty Crocker Kitchens seal guarantees success in your kitchen. Every recipe has been tested in America's Most Trusted Kitchens™ to meet our high standards of reliability, easy preparation and great taste.

Dear Friends,

Comfort food is more popular than ever and for good reason! Simple and straightforward, these recipes are sure to please time and again—invoking fond memories with each bite.

You'll find plenty of your favorites here. If you love cheese (and who doesn't?), there's a whole chapter of cheesy favorites. Turn to the chapter of breakfast foods anytime on those days when you just want to wear your robe and slippers around the house.

And that's only the beginning. We've taken comfort food a step further with a chapter on comfort foods that are good for you as well as tasty.

You can't go wrong with any of these delicious choices. Take comfort in their heartiness and savor the new memories you are sure to make while enjoying them with friends and family.

Warmly,

Betty Crocker

contents

Feel-Good Foods

Warm, welcoming and great to come home to—we've taken classic home cooking and added a delicious twist!

Not Your Mom's Mac 'n' Cheese

Start with Betty's tried-and-true Grandma's Macaroni and Cheese (page 56). Then try one of these variations—or try a few different add-ins to create your own unique mac 'n' cheese! Tip: Save time and buy the cheese that's already shredded. Worth a second helping? You bet!

1   Grab a different cheese, or two

>   1 cup shredded peppered Monterey Jack (4 ounces)
>   + 1 cup shredded sharp Cheddar cheese (4 ounces).

>   1 cup shredded Swiss cheese (4 ounces)
>   + 1 cup shredded sharp Cheddar cheese (4 ounces).

>   2 cups shredded Mexican cheese (8 ounces) instead of Cheddar.

>   2 cups shredded Italian cheese (8 ounces), instead of Cheddar.

2   Add some cooked veggies

>   Cooked green peas and sautéed chopped sweet red pepper.

3   Toss in a little meat

>   Crisp crumbled bacon.

>   Diced cooked ham.

>   Small bites of pepperoni, salami or pastrami.

Grilled Cheese—Your Way!

Nothing says comfort like a grilled American cheese sandwich. To prepare, follow Step 3 of Onion and Bacon Grilled Cheese sandwiches (page 118) using these fresh takes. (Tip: For even browning, weigh it down as it cooks with a bacon press or small flat skillet like many short-order chefs use.)

Double the Cheese Cheddar and Muenster on sourdough.

Le Déjeuner Ham & Brie on croissant with Dijon mustard.

Wall-Streeter roast beef & Havarti on country white.

The Alpine Smoked turkey & Gruyère on 5-grain.

Midwestern Cheddar & Maytag Blue on cracked wheat.

Southwestern Special Monterey Jack–Colby on whole wheat. Serve with salsa.

Many Sides to Mashed Potatoes

Make them as a side dish, or enjoy as your main dish. See Betty's never-fail steps to mashing them on page 60, and stir in one of these extras at the end.

For Garlic Lovers Add smashed roasted garlic and a sprinkling of cracked black pepper.

Green and White Top with cooked fresh broccoli florets and shreds of Cheddar.

Olé! Add heated-up taco sauce, chopped green onions and shredded Mexican cheese.

The Tuscan Stir in crumbled Gorgonzola and toasted walnuts.

Bon Appetito! Blend in shredded mozzarella and bits of pepperoni.

Pasta Tonight!

TGIP—thank goodness, it's pasta! To make it fast, start with fresh pasta; you'll only need to cook it for a few minutes (usually about 3 to 5 minutes according to the package). Try different shapes and sizes, then stir in one of these:

- Crumbled Gorgonzola and toasted walnuts.
- Peppered Brie, halved grape tomatoes and grated Romano.
- Chopped plum tomatoes, smoked mozzarella and snipped fresh basil.
- Crisp crumbled bacon, shredded fresh Parmesan and a little whipping cream.

Frosty Treats!

Start with yogurt or ice cream and whirl up a smoothie. Instant comfort!

- **Creamsicle Smoothie** $1/2$ pint vanilla ice cream + 2 tablespoons frozen (thawed) orange juice concentrate + 1 tablespoon milk. Just blend . . . and it's ready.

- **Fresh Berry Smoothie** $1/3$ cup strawberry (or raspberry) yogurt + $1/2$ cup fresh strawberries (or raspberries) + $1/4$ cup whole milk. Blend until the berries disappear and the drink turns pink.

- **The Carribean** 1 container (6 ounces) strawberry mango yogurt + $1/2$ cup sliced fresh strawberries + $1/2$ cup pineapple juice. Blend until smooth, then pour into a chilled glass and float a fresh strawberry on top.

- **Chocolate Malted** $1/3$ cup milk + 2 tablespoons chocolate-flavored syrup + 2 teaspoon chocolate-flavored malted milk powder + 1 pint chocolate ice cream. Pour into a tall soda glass and drink it icy cold. (Tip: Blend the first three ingredients with a little ice cream until smooth, then add in the rest of the ice cream.)

Make Mine Hot Fudge!

Scoop up a sundae, just like at the ice cream shop—then dive in!

Hot Fudge Sundae: Spoon some thick hot fudge sauce (warmed in the microwave or on the stove over low heat) into a sundae glass or large bowl, scoop in lots of vanilla or chocolate ice cream, add more hot fudge, and sprinkle on toasted pecans. Top with lots of chocolate sprinkles and swirl on whipped cream.

Brownie Sundae: Start with a brownie, then top with vanilla or coffee ice cream, hot fudge ice cream topping (warmed in the microwave or on the stove over low heat), and dry roasted peanuts. Swirl on whipped cream.

Fresh Strawberry Sundae: Spoon in one scoop of vanilla ice cream and another of strawberry ice cream. Drizzle on some strawberry ice cream topping or melted strawberry jelly, cover with sliced fresh strawberries and sprinkle with chopped toasted almonds. Swirl on whipped cream.

Rocky Road: Start with a couple of scoops of fudge ripple ice cream, spoon on some chocolate ice cream topping, then add marshmallow fluff. Shower with miniature marshmallows and dry-roasted peanuts. Swirl whipped cream on the top.

1

breakfast anytime

Easy Cream Drop Biscuits

Prep Time: 15 min ▪ Start to Finish: 30 min ▪ 12 Biscuits

1³/₄ cups all-purpose flour
2¹/₂ teaspoons baking powder
¹/₂ teaspoon salt
1¹/₃ cups whipping cream

1 Heat oven to 450°F. Grease cookie sheet with shortening or spray with cooking spray. In large bowl, mix flour, baking powder and salt. Stir in whipping cream just until blended and a dough forms. Add 1 to 2 tablespoons additional cream if dough is very thick.

2 Drop dough by 12 spoonfuls onto cookie sheet.

3 Bake 10 to 12 minutes or until bottoms are golden brown. Immediately remove from cookie sheet. Serve warm.

1 Biscuit: Calories 150 (Calories from Fat 80); Total Fat 8g (Saturated Fat 5g); Cholesterol 30mg; Sodium 210mg; Total Carbohydrate 15g (Dietary Fiber 0g); Protein 2g

Buttermilk-Herb Biscuits

Prep Time: 15 min ■ Start to Finish: 25 min ■ About 12 Biscuits

2 cups all-purpose flour
2 teaspoons baking powder
1½ teaspoons dried herb leaves, such as rosemary, basil or thyme,
    or Italian seasoning
½ teaspoon salt
½ teaspoon baking soda
⅓ cup shortening
1 cup buttermilk
1 tablespoon butter or margarine, melted

1 Heat oven to 400°F. In medium bowl, mix flour, baking powder, herbs, salt and baking soda. Cut in shortening, using pastry blender (or pulling 2 table knives through ingredients in opposite directions), until mixture looks like fine crumbs. Stir in buttermilk until dough leaves side of bowl (dough will be soft and sticky).

2 On lightly floured surface, lightly knead dough 10 times. Roll or pat dough about 1 inch thick. Cut with floured 2-inch cutter. On ungreased cookie sheet, place biscuits about 1 inch apart. Brush with butter.

3 Bake 14 to 16 minutes or until golden brown. Immediately remove from cookie sheet. Serve warm.

1 Biscuit: Calories 140 (Calories from Fat 70); Total Fat 7g (Saturated Fat 2.5g); Cholesterol 0mg; Sodium 260mg; Total Carbohydrate 17g (Dietary Fiber 0g); Protein 3g

Blueberry Muffins

Prep Time: 10 min ▪ Start to Finish: 40 min ▪ 12 Muffins

3/4 cup milk
1/4 cup vegetable oil
1 large egg
2 cups all-purpose flour*
1/2 cup sugar
2 teaspoons baking powder
1/2 teaspoon salt
1 cup fresh, canned (drained) or frozen blueberries

1 Heat oven to 400°F. Grease bottoms only of 12 medium muffin cups with shortening, spray with cooking spray or line with paper baking cups.

2 In large bowl, beat milk, oil and egg with fork or wire whisk until well mixed. Stir in flour, sugar, baking powder and salt all at once just until flour is moistened (batter will be lumpy). Fold in blueberries. Divide batter evenly among muffin cups.

3 Bake 20 to 25 minutes or until golden brown. If baked in greased pan, let stand about 5 minutes in pan, then remove from pan to wire rack; if baked in paper baking cups, immediately remove from pan to wire rack. Serve warm if desired.

*If using self-rising flour, omit baking powder and salt.

Mix it up – make Cranberry Orange Muffins: Omit the blueberries and beat in 1 tablespoon grated orange peel with the milk. Fold 1 cup coarsely chopped cranberries into batter.

1 Muffin: Calories 170 (Calories from Fat 50); Total Fat 6g (Saturated Fat 1g); Cholesterol 20mg; Sodium 190mg; Total Carbohydrate 27g (Dietary Fiber 0g); Protein 3g

On-the-Go Apple Breakfast Bars

Prep Time: 30 min ▪ Start to Finish: 2 hrs 30 min ▪ 16 Bars

1¹/₂ cups dried apples,
    finely chopped
¹/₂ cup chopped pecans
2¹/₂ cups Whole Grain Total® cereal
¹/₃ cup honey
¹/₂ cup golden raisins
1 tablespoon packed brown sugar

¹/₃ cup chunky or creamy
    peanut butter
¹/₂ cup apple butter
¹/₂ teaspoon ground cinnamon
¹/₂ cup quick-cooking or old-fashioned oats
¹/₂ cup roasted sunflower nuts

1 Line bottom and sides of 8-inch square pan with foil; spray with cooking spray. Sprinkle ¹/₂ cup of the apples and ¹/₄ cup of the pecans over bottom of pan. Place cereal in food-storage plastic bag or between sheets of waxed paper; coarsely crush with rolling pin (or coarsely crush in blender or food processor); set aside.

2 In 4-quart Dutch oven, heat ¹/₂ cup of the apples, the honey, raisins and brown sugar to boiling over medium-high heat, stirring occasionally. Reduce heat to medium. Cook uncovered about 1 minute, stirring constantly, until hot and bubbly; remove from heat.

3 Stir peanut butter into cooked mixture until melted. Stir in apple butter and cinnamon. Stir in oats, sunflower nuts and ¹/₄ cup of the pecans until well mixed. Stir in crushed cereal.

4 Press mixture very firmly (or bars will crumble) and evenly onto apples and pecans in pan. Sprinkle with remaining ¹/₂ cup apples and ¹/₄ cup pecans; press lightly into bars. Refrigerate about 2 hours or until set. For bars, cut into 8 rows by 2 rows. Store covered in refrigerator.

1 Bar: Calories 180 (Calories from Fat 70); Total Fat 8g (Saturated Fat 1g); Cholesterol 0mg; Sodium 85mg; Total Carbohydrate 25g (Dietary Fiber 3g); Protein 3g

Cranberry-Pecan Granola

Prep Time: 35 min ▪ Start to Finish: 35 min ▪ 8 Servings (³/₄ cup each)

3 cups old-fashioned oats
¹/₄ cup chopped pecans
¹/₄ cup frozen orange juice concentrate, thawed
¹/₄ cup real maple syrup or maple-flavored syrup
¹/₂ teaspoon ground cinnamon
2 teaspoons canola oil
2 cups Wheat Chex® cereal
1¹/₃ cups sweetened dried cranberries (about 6 oz)

1 Heat oven to 325°F. In large bowl, mix oats and pecans.

2 In small bowl, mix juice concentrate, syrup, cinnamon and oil until well blended. Drizzle over oat mixture; toss well to coat evenly. Stir in cereal. Spread on 2 large cookie sheets or in 2 (15×10×1-inch) pans.

3 Bake 20 to 25 minutes, stirring granola frequently and changing positions of cookie sheets once halfway through baking, until light golden brown. Stir half of cranberries into each half of granola.

Sure, this granola makes a wonderful breakfast, but it's also a scrumptious snack—tote it along whenever you want a nutritious nosh.

1 Serving: Calories 310 (Calories from Fat 50); Total Fat 6g (Saturated Fat 0.5g); Cholesterol 0mg; Sodium 110mg; Total Carbohydrate 58g (Dietary Fiber 6g); Protein 7g

Triple-Berry Oatmeal Muesli

Prep Time: 25 min ▪ Start to Finish: 40 min ▪ 6 Servings

2³/₄ cups old-fashioned oats or barley flakes
¹/₂ cup sliced almonds
2 containers (6 oz each) banana crème low-fat yogurt
1¹/₂ cups fat-free (skim) milk
¹/₄ cup ground flaxseed or flaxseed meal
¹/₂ cup fresh blueberries
¹/₂ cup fresh raspberries
¹/₂ cup sliced fresh strawberries

1 Heat oven to 350°F. On cookie sheet, spread oats and almonds. Bake 18 to 20 minutes, stirring occasionally, until light golden brown; cool 15 minutes.

2 In large bowl, mix yogurt and milk until well blended. Stir in oats, almonds and flaxseed. Top each serving with berries.

This tastes great—and has a healthy dose of flaxseed!

1 Serving: Calories 310 (Calories from Fat 80); Total Fat 9g (Saturated Fat 1.5g); Cholesterol 0mg; Sodium 60mg; Total Carbohydrate 46g (Dietary Fiber 8g); Protein 13g

Puffy Oven Pancake with Berries

Prep Time: 10 min ▪ Start to Finish: 40 min ▪ 4 Servings

2 tablespoons butter or margarine
3 eggs or 6 egg whites
$\frac{1}{2}$ cup all-purpose flour
$\frac{1}{2}$ cup fat-free (skim) milk
$\frac{1}{4}$ teaspoon salt
$2\frac{1}{2}$ cups assorted fresh berries
Powdered sugar, if desired

1 Heat oven to 400°F. In 9-inch glass pie plate, melt butter in oven; brush butter over bottom and side of pie plate.

2 In medium bowl, beat eggs slightly with wire whisk or hand beater. Beat in flour, milk and salt just until mixed (do not over beat). Pour into pie plate.

3 Bake 25 to 30 minutes or until puffy and deep golden brown. Serve pancake immediately topped with berries. Sprinkle with powdered sugar.

1 Serving: Calories 220 (Calories from Fat 90); Total Fat 10g (Saturated Fat 5g); Cholesterol 175mg; Sodium 250mg; Total Carbohydrate 24g (Dietary Fiber 3g); Protein 8g

Nothing is cozier than pancakes—put on your slippers and cook up a batch.

Blueberry-Orange Pancakes with Blueberry-Orange Sauce

Prep Time: 35 min ▪ Start to Finish: 35 min ▪ 7 Servings (2 pancakes each)

Blueberry-Orange Sauce
¼ cup sugar
1½ teaspoons cornstarch
2 tablespoons orange juice
¼ teaspoon grated orange peel
2 cups fresh or frozen unsweetened
   blueberries

Pancakes
2 cups Original Bisquick® mix
1 cup fat-free (skim) milk
2 eggs or ½ cup fat-free egg product
1 teaspoon grated orange peel
¼ teaspoon ground nutmeg
1 cup fresh or frozen unsweetened
   blueberries

1 In 1½-quart saucepan, mix sugar and cornstarch. Stir in orange juice and ¼ teaspoon orange peel until smooth. Stir in 2 cups blueberries. Heat to boiling over medium heat, stirring constantly. Boil about 2 minutes, stirring occasionally, until thickened. Keep warm while making pancakes.

2 Heat griddle or skillet over medium heat or to 375°F. Grease griddle with canola oil if necessary (or spray with cooking spray before heating).

3 In medium bowl, stir all pancake ingredients except blueberries with spoon until blended. Fold in 1 cup blueberries. For each pancake, pour slightly less than ¼ cup batter onto hot griddle. Cook until edges are dry. Turn; cook other sides until golden. Serve with warm sauce.

1 Serving: Calories 230 (Calories from Fat 60); Total Fat 7g (Saturated Fat 1.5g); Cholesterol 60mg; Sodium 530mg; Total Carbohydrate 40g (Dietary Fiber 2g); Protein 6g

The berry sauce is delicious—but if you don't have time to make it, regular syrup works just as well.

Monte Cristo Stuffed French Toast with Strawberry Syrup

Prep Time: 20 min ▪ Start to Finish: 20 min ▪ 3 Servings (2 sandwiches each)

12 slices French bread, 1/2 inch thick
1/4 lb shaved or very thinly sliced cooked ham
3 slices (1 oz each) Gruyère or Swiss cheese, cut in half
3 eggs
1/2 cup milk
2 tablespoons granulated sugar
1 tablespoon butter or margarine
Powdered sugar, if desired
3/4 cup strawberry syrup

1 Top 6 slices of the bread evenly with ham and cheese, folding to fit. Top with remaining bread slices.

2 In small bowl, beat eggs, milk and granulated sugar with fork or wire whisk until well mixed; pour into shallow bowl.

3 In 12-inch nonstick skillet, heat butter over medium-low heat. Dip each side of each sandwich in egg mixture, allowing time for bread to soak up mixture. Add sandwiches to skillet. Cover; cook 2 to 3 minutes on each side or until golden brown. Sprinkle with powdered sugar. Serve with syrup.

1 Serving: Calories 850 (Calories from Fat 200); Total Fat 22g (Saturated Fat 10g); Cholesterol 265mg; Sodium 1360mg; Total Carbohydrate 132g (Dietary Fiber 3g); Protein 31g

Belgian Waffles
with Berry Cream

Prep Time: 15 min ▪ Start to Finish: 15 min ▪ 12 Servings (1 waffle each)

Berry Cream

1 cup whipping cream

$1/4$ cup powdered sugar

2 cups sliced fresh strawberries or
    1 package (10 oz) sliced frozen
    strawberries, thawed, drained

$1/2$ cup fresh or frozen (thawed and
    drained) blueberries

Waffles

2 eggs

1 cup milk

$2^{1}/_{3}$ cups Original Bisquick mix

2 tablespoons granulated sugar

$1/4$ cup vegetable oil

Additional berries, if desired

1 In chilled medium bowl, beat whipping cream and powdered sugar with electric mixer on high speed until stiff peaks form. Fold in strawberries and blueberries.

2 Heat Belgian or regular waffle iron. (Waffle irons without a nonstick coating may need to be brushed with vegetable oil or sprayed with cooking spray before batter for each waffle is added.)

3 In small bowl, beat eggs with electric mixer on high speed about 3 minutes or until thick and lemon colored. Beat in milk. Beat in Bisquick and granulated sugar on low speed until smooth. Gently fold in oil. Pour batter onto hot waffle iron. (Check manufacturer's directions for recommended amount of batter.) Close lid of waffle iron.

4 Bake about 5 minutes or until steaming stops. Carefully remove waffle. Top each waffle with berry cream and additional berries.

Is this breakfast or dessert? You decide!

1 Serving: Calories 250 (Calories from Fat 140); Total Fat 15g (Saturated Fat 6g); Cholesterol 60mg; Sodium 360mg; Total Carbohydrate 23g (Dietary Fiber 0g); Protein 4g

Easy Huevos Rancheros

Prep Time: 25 min ▪ Start to Finish: 25 min ▪ 2 Servings

2 flour tortillas (7 or 8 inch)
1 can (8 oz) tomato sauce
1/4 cup salsa
1/4 teaspoon sugar
1/4 teaspoon ground cumin
1 clove garlic, finely chopped
4 eggs
1/4 cup shredded
Colby–Monterey Jack cheese blend (1 oz)

1 Heat oven to 350°F. Wrap tortillas in aluminum foil. Heat about 10 minutes until warm. Remove tortillas from oven; keep wrapped.

2 Meanwhile, mix tomato sauce, salsa, sugar, cumin and garlic in 1-quart saucepan. Heat to boiling; reduce heat. Cover and simmer 5 minutes, stirring occasionally.

3 Heat water (1 1/2 to 2 inches) to boiling in 10-inch skillet; reduce heat to low. Break each egg, one at a time, into custard cup or saucer. Hold cup or saucer close to water's surface and slip egg into water. Cook uncovered 6 to 7 minutes or until whites are set and yolks are thickened. Remove eggs with slotted spoon.

4 Place each warm tortilla on dinner plate. Top each tortilla with 2 poached eggs and the sauce. Sprinkle with cheese.

Huevos Rancheros ("ranch-style eggs") refers to any egg dish served on tortillas. If you prefer, you can fry the eggs instead of poaching them.

1 Serving: Calories 390 (Calories from Fat 170); Total Fat 19g (Saturated Fat 7g); Cholesterol 440mg; Sodium 1300mg; Total Carbohydrate 37g (Dietary Fiber 4g); Protein 22g

Breakfast Burritos

Prep Time: 20 min ▪ Start to Finish: 20 min ▪ 4 Burritos

1 tablespoon butter or margarine
4 medium green onions, sliced (1/4 cup)
1 1/2 medium green, red or yellow bell peppers, chopped (1 1/2 cups)
6 eggs
2 tablespoons milk
1/2 teaspoon salt
1/4 teaspoon pepper
4 flour tortillas (7 or 8 inches in diameter), heated
1/2 cup shredded Monterey Jack cheese with jalapeño peppers (2 oz)

1 Melt butter in 10-inch nonstick skillet over medium-high heat. Cook onions and bell peppers in butter 2 to 3 minutes, stirring occasionally, until crisp-tender.

2 Beat eggs, milk, salt and pepper in medium bowl with fork or wire whisk until well mixed. Pour egg mixture over vegetables in skillet. Reduce heat to medium. Cook 4 to 6 minutes, stirring frequently, until eggs are set but still moist.

3 Spoon egg mixture onto warm tortillas; sprinkle with cheese. Roll up tortillas.

1 Burrito: Calories 320 (Calories from Fat 160); Total Fat 18g (Saturated Fat 8g); Cholesterol 340mg; Sodium 640mg; Total Carbohydrate 23g (Dietary Fiber 2g); Protein 17g

Potato, Bacon and Egg Scramble

Prep Time: 25 min ▪ Start to Finish: 25 min ▪ 5 Servings

5 slices bacon	¼ teaspoon salt
1 lb small red potatoes (6 or 7), cubed	⅛ teaspoon pepper
6 eggs	2 tablespoons butter or margarine
⅓ cup milk	4 medium green onions, sliced (¼ cup)

1 In 10-inch skillet, cook bacon over medium heat 8 to 10 minutes, turning occasionally, until crisp and brown. Remove, drain on paper towels, and crumble.

2 Meanwhile, in 2-quart saucepan, heat 1 inch water to boiling. Add potatoes. Cover; heat to boiling. Reduce heat to medium-low. Cook covered 6 to 8 minutes or until potatoes are tender; drain. In medium bowl, beat eggs, milk, salt and pepper with fork or wire whisk until well mixed; set aside.

3 In 10-inch skillet, melt butter over medium-high heat. Cook potatoes in butter 3 to 5 minutes, turning potatoes occasionally, until light brown. Stir in onions. Cook 1 minute, stirring constantly.

4 Pour egg mixture into skillet. As mixture begins to set at bottom and side, gently lift cooked portions with metal spatula so that thin, uncooked portion can flow to bottom. Avoid constant stirring. Cook 3 to 4 minutes or until eggs are thickened throughout but still moist. Sprinkle with crumbled bacon.

Go ahead and make this even easier—buy refrigerated cubed potatoes.

1 Serving: Calories 260 (Calories from Fat 130); Total Fat 15g (Saturated Fat 6g); Cholesterol 275mg; Sodium 420mg; Total Carbohydrate 18g (Dietary Fiber 2g); Protein 13g

Extra-Moist Scrambled Eggs with Chives

Prep Time: 10 min ■ Start to Finish: 15 min ■ 4 Servings

6 eggs
1 tablespoon chopped fresh chives
1/4 teaspoon salt
1/8 teaspoon pepper, if desired
1/2 cup milk or half-and-half
3 tablespoons butter

1 In medium bowl, beat eggs, chives, salt and pepper with fork or wire whisk until well mixed.

2 In 10-inch skillet, heat milk and butter over medium heat just until butter melts and liquid is steaming. Pour egg mixture into skillet.

3 As mixture heats, portions of eggs will begin to set. Gently push cooked portions with metal spatula to the outside edge of skillet. Avoid stirring constantly. As more egg sets, push it to the edge as well and stack it on top of the set egg mixture already there. Cook 5 to 6 minutes or until eggs are thickened throughout but still moist.

The fresh chives really make this dish special—it's worth a trip to the store.

1 Serving: Calories 210 (Calories from Fat 150); Total Fat 17g (Saturated Fat 7g); Cholesterol 345mg; Sodium 310mg; Total Carbohydrate 2g (Dietary Fiber 0g); Protein 11g

Bacon, Cheese and Tomato Strata

Prep Time: 15 min ▪ Start to Finish: 3 hrs 15 min ▪ 12 Servings

7 cups lightly packed 1-inch cubes French bread (8 oz)
2 cups shredded reduced-fat Cheddar cheese (8 oz)
2 cups chopped plum (Roma) tomatoes (6 medium)
6 eggs or 1 1/2 cups fat-free egg product
1 1/2 cups fat-free (skim) milk
1 teaspoon Dijon mustard
1 teaspoon dried basil leaves
1/2 teaspoon salt
6 slices bacon

1 Spray 13×9-inch (3-quart) glass baking dish with cooking spray. Spread bread in baking dish. Sprinkle evenly with 1 1/2 cups of the cheese; mix lightly with bread. Sprinkle with tomatoes.

2 In medium bowl, beat eggs, milk, mustard, basil and salt with fork or wire whisk; pour over bread mixture. Cover tightly and refrigerate at least 2 hours but no longer than 24 hours.

3 Heat oven to 350°F. Bake uncovered 40 to 45 minutes or until knife inserted in center comes out clean. Meanwhile, in 10-inch skillet, cook bacon over medium heat 8 to 10 minutes, turning occasionally, until crisp; drain on paper towel.

4 Crumble bacon. Sprinkle bacon and remaining 1/2 cup cheese over strata. Let stand 10 minutes before serving.

1 Serving: Calories 160 (Calories from Fat 60); Total Fat 7g (Saturated Fat 2.5g); Cholesterol 115mg; Sodium 510mg; Total Carbohydrate 13g (Dietary Fiber 0g); Protein 12g

Denver Omelet

Prep Time: 16 min ▪ Start to Finish: 16 min ▪ 1 Serving

2 teaspoons butter or margarine
2 tablespoons chopped fully cooked ham
1 tablespoon finely chopped bell pepper
1 tablespoon finely chopped onion
2 eggs, beaten

1 Heat butter in 8-inch omelet pan or skillet over medium-high heat just until butter begins to brown. As butter melts, tilt pan to coat bottom. Cook ham, bell pepper and onion in butter 2 minutes, stirring frequently.

2 Quickly pour eggs into pan. While sliding pan back and forth rapidly over heat, quickly stir with fork to spread eggs continuously over bottom of pan as they thicken. Let stand over heat a few seconds to lightly brown bottom of omelet. (Do not overcook—omelet will continue to cook after folding.)

3 Tilt pan and run fork under edge of omelet, then jerk pan sharply to loosen eggs from bottom of pan. Fold portion of omelet nearest you just to center. (Allow for portion of omelet to slide up side of pan.) Turn omelet onto warm plate, flipping folded portion of omelet over so it rolls over the bottom. Tuck sides of omelet under if necessary.

Cheese lovers only! Lose the ham, bell pepper and onion, and sprinkle the omelet with 1/4 cup shredded Cheddar, Monterey Jack or Swiss cheese or 1/4 cup crumbled blue cheese before folding.

1 Serving: Calories 260 (Calories from Fat 180); Total Fat 20g (Saturated Fat 9g); Cholesterol 455mg; Sodium 430mg; Total Carbohydrate 3g (Dietary Fiber 0g); Protein 17g

English Muffin Breakfast Pizzas

Prep Time: 20 min ▪ Start to Finish: 20 min ▪ 4 Servings

1 cup fat-free egg product or 4 eggs
1/4 cup fat-free (skim) milk
Dash of salt
Dash of pepper
2 teaspoons canola or soybean oil
2 tablespoons chopped onion
2 tablespoons chopped red bell pepper
2 tablespoons chopped cooked ham
1/2 cup shredded reduced-fat Cheddar cheese (2 oz)
2 whole wheat English muffins, split, toasted

1 In small bowl, beat egg product, milk, salt and pepper with wire whisk or fork until well blended.

2 In 10-inch nonstick skillet, heat oil over medium heat. Cook onion, bell pepper and ham in oil 3 to 5 minutes, stirring occasionally, until vegetables are crisp-tender. Pour egg mixture into skillet. As eggs begin to set at bottom and side, gently lift cooked portions with spatula so that uncooked egg can flow to bottom. Cook 3 to 4 minutes or until eggs are thickened throughout but still moist; stir cheese into eggs.

3 Spoon egg mixture evenly over muffin halves.

1 Serving: Calories 150 (Calories from Fat 40); Total Fat 4.5g (Saturated Fat 1g); Cholesterol 5mg; Sodium 570mg; Total Carbohydrate 16g (Dietary Fiber 3g); Protein 14g

2
comfort classics

Split Pea Soup

Prep Time: 20 min ▪ Start to Finish: 2 hrs ▪ 8 Servings

2¼ cups dried split peas (1 lb), sorted and rinsed
8 cups water
¼ teaspoon pepper
1 large onion, chopped (1 cup)
2 medium stalks celery, finely chopped (1 cup)
1 ham bone, 2 lb ham shanks or 2 lb smoked pork hocks
3 medium carrots, cut into ¼-inch slices (1½ cups)

1 In 4-quart Dutch oven, heat all ingredients except carrots to boiling, stirring occasionally; reduce heat. Cover and simmer 1 hour to 1 hour 30 minutes.

2 Remove ham bone; let stand until cool enough to handle. Remove ham from bone. Remove excess fat from ham; cut ham into ½-inch pieces.

3 Stir ham and carrots into soup. Heat to boiling; reduce heat. Cover and simmer about 30 minutes or until carrots are tender and soup is desired consistency.

Slow Cooker Directions: Decrease water to 7 cups. In 4- to 6-quart slow cooker, mix all ingredients. Cover and cook on low heat setting 3 to 4 hours or until peas are tender. Remove ham bone; let stand until cool enough to handle. Remove excess fat from ham; cut ham into ½-inch pieces. Stir ham into soup.

1 Serving: Calories 250 (Calories from Fat 60); Total Fat 6g (Saturated Fat 2g); Cholesterol 15mg; Sodium 250mg; Total Carbohydrate 32g (Dietary Fiber 16g); Protein 16g

Chicken Noodle Soup

Prep Time: 55 min ▪ Start to Finish: 1 hr 55 min ▪ 6 Servings

Chicken and Broth
1 cut-up whole chicken (3 to 3½ lb)
4½ cups cold water
1 teaspoon salt
½ teaspoon pepper
1 medium celery stalk (with leaves), cut-up
1 carrot, cut up
1 small onion, cut up
1 parsley sprig

Soup
2 medium carrots, sliced (1 cup)
2 medium celery stalks, sliced (1 cup)
1 small onion, chopped (¼ cup)
1 tablespoon chicken bouillon
　　granules
1 cup uncooked medium egg
　　noodles (2 oz)
Chopped fresh parsley

1 Remove excess fat from chicken. In Dutch oven or stock pot, place chicken, giblets (except liver) and neck. Add remaining chicken and broth ingredients; heat to boiling. Skim foam from broth; reduce heat to low. Cover and simmer about 45 minutes or until juice of chicken is no longer pink when centers of thickest pieces are cut.

2 Remove chicken from broth. Cool chicken about 10 minutes or just until cool enough to handle. Strain broth through cheesecloth-lined strainer; discard vegetables. Remove skin and bones from chicken. Cut chicken into ½-inch pieces. Skim and discard fat from broth. Use immediately, or cover and refrigerate broth and chicken in separate containers up to 24 hours or freeze for future use.

3 Add enough water to broth to measure 5 cups. In Dutch oven, heat broth, sliced carrots, sliced celery, chopped onion and bouillon granules to boiling. Reduce heat to low; cover and simmer about 15 minutes or until carrots are tender.

4 Stir in noodles and chicken. Heat to boiling. Reduce heat to low; simmer uncovered 7 to 10 minutes or until noodles are tender, stirring occasionally. Sprinkle with parsley.

1 Serving: Calories 190 (Calories from Fat 55); Total Fat 6g (Saturated Fat 2g); Cholesterol 80mg; Sodium 1120mg; Total Carbohydrate 10g (Dietary Fiber 1g); Protein 25g

Chunky Tomato Soup

Prep Time: 15 min ▪ Start to Finish: 1 hr 35 min ▪ 8 Servings (1½ cups each)

2 tablespoons olive or vegetable oil
2 cloves garlic, finely chopped
2 medium stalks celery, coarsely chopped (1 cup)
2 medium carrots, coarsely chopped (1 cup)
2 cans (28 oz each) Italian-style peeled whole tomatoes, undrained
2 cups water
1 teaspoon dried basil leaves
¼ teaspoon pepper
2 cans (14 oz each) chicken broth

1 Heat oil in 5- to 6-quart Dutch oven over medium-high heat. Cook garlic, celery and carrots in oil 5 to 7 minutes, stirring frequently, until carrots are crisp-tender.

2 Stir in tomatoes, breaking up tomatoes coarsely. Stir in water, basil, pepper and broth. Heat to boiling; reduce heat to low.

3 Cover and simmer 1 hour, stirring occasionally.

Go totally veggie—use two 14-ounce cans of vegetable broth instead of the chicken broth.

1 Serving: Calories 95 (Calories from Fat 35); Total Fat 4g (Saturated Fat 1g); Cholesterol 0mg; Sodium 760mg; Total Carbohydrate 11g (Dietary Fiber 3g); Protein 4g

Home-Style Chicken and Dumplings

Prep Time: 15 min ▪ Start to Finish: 6 hrs 50 min ▪ 4 Servings

1 large potato, peeled, cut into
  ¹/₂-inch pieces (1¹/₂ cups)
2 medium carrots, sliced (1 cup)
1 can (14 oz) chicken broth
¹/₄ cup all-purpose flour
1 teaspoon salt
¹/₂ teaspoon dried marjoram leaves

¹/₄ teaspoon pepper
2 lb boneless skinless chicken thighs
1 box (9 oz) frozen baby sweet peas, thawed
1¹/₂ cups Original Bisquick mix
¹/₂ cup milk
Paprika, if desired

1 In 3¹/₂- to 4-quart slow cooker, place potato and carrots. In medium bowl, mix broth, flour, salt, marjoram and pepper; pour into cooker. Add chicken.

2 Cover; cook on low heat setting 6 to 7 hours.

3 Stir in peas. Increase heat setting to high. Cover; cook 15 minutes.

4 In small bowl, stir Bisquick mix and milk until Bisquick mix is moistened. Drop dough by spoonfuls onto chicken mixture. Sprinkle with paprika. Cover; cook on high heat setting about 20 minutes or until toothpick inserted in center of dumplings comes out clean.

Keep it simple—use packaged sliced carrots to save on Prep Time.

1 Serving: Calories 700 (Calories from Fat 230); Total Fat 26g (Saturated Fat 8g); Cholesterol 145mg; Sodium 1870mg; Total Carbohydrate 57g (Dietary Fiber 5g); Protein 59g

Creamy Herbed Chicken Stew

Prep Time: 30 min ▪ Start to Finish: 8 hrs 40 min ▪ 12 Servings (1¹/₂ cups each)

4 cups baby-cut carrots

4 medium Yukon gold potatoes, cut into 1¹/₂-inch pieces

1 large onion, chopped (1 cup)

2 medium stalks celery, sliced (1 cup)

1 teaspoon dried thyme leaves

¹/₂ teaspoon salt

¹/₂ teaspoon pepper

2 pounds boneless, skinless chicken thighs

3 cups chicken broth

2 cups fresh snap pea pods

1 cup whipping cream

¹/₂ cup all-purpose flour

1 teaspoon dried thyme leaves

1 Place carrots, potatoes, onion and celery in 5- to 6-quart slow cooker. Sprinkle with 1 teaspoon thyme, the salt and pepper. Top with chicken and broth.

2 Cover and cook on low heat setting 7 to 8 hours, adding pea pods for last 5 to 10 minutes of cooking.

3 Remove chicken and vegetables from cooker to serving bowl, using slotted spoon; cover to keep warm. Increase heat setting to high. Mix whipping cream, flour and 1 teaspoon thyme in small bowl; stir into liquid in cooker. Cover and cook about 10 minutes or until thickened. Pour sauce over chicken and vegetables.

1 Serving: Calories 270 (Calories from Fat 110); Total Fat 13g (Saturated Fat 6g); Cholesterol 70mg; Sodium 430mg; Total Carbohydrate 19g (Dietary Fiber 3g); Protein 20g

Chicken Pot Pie

Prep Time: 14 min ■ Start to Finish: 44 min ■ 10 Servings

2 cans (10³/₄ oz each) condensed cream of chicken and mushroom soup
1 can (10³/₄ oz) condensed chicken broth
4 cups cut-up cooked chicken
1 bag (1 lb) frozen mixed vegetables, thawed and drained
2 cups Original Bisquick mix
1¹/₂ cups milk
¹/₂ teaspoon poultry seasoning

1 Heat oven to 375°F (350°F for glass baking dish). Heat soup, broth, chicken and vegetables to boiling in 3-quart saucepan, stirring constantly. Boil and stir 1 minute. Spread in ungreased rectangular pan, 13×9×2 inches.

2 Stir together remaining ingredients. Pour over chicken mixture.

3 Bake uncovered about 30 minutes or until light brown.

It's hard to believe that comfort food could be so easy—it's homemade heaven!

1 Serving: Calories 285 (Calories from Fat 110); Total Fat 12g (Saturated Fat 4g); Cholesterol 55mg; Sodium 1040mg; Total Carbohydrate 24g (Dietary Fiber 2g); Protein 22g

Turkey and Corn Bread Casserole

Prep Time: 25 min ▪ Start to Finish: 1 hr 40 min ▪ 6 Servings

2 tablespoons butter or margarine
1 medium onion, chopped ($^1/_2$ cup)
1 small red bell pepper, chopped ($^1/_2$ cup)
4 cups seasoned corn bread stuffing mix
1 cup frozen whole kernel corn (from 1-lb bag)
$1^1/_2$ cups water
2 turkey breast tenderloins (about $^3/_4$ lb each)
$^1/_2$ teaspoon chili powder
$^1/_2$ teaspoon peppered seasoned salt

1 Heat oven to 350°F. Spray 11×7-inch (2-quart) glass baking dish with cooking spray. In 12-inch nonstick skillet, melt butter over medium-high heat. Cook onion and bell pepper in butter 2 to 3 minutes, stirring frequently, until tender. Stir in stuffing mix, corn and water. Spread stuffing mixture in baking dish.

2 Sprinkle both sides of turkey tenderloins with chili powder and peppered seasoned salt. Place on stuffing, pressing into stuffing mixture slightly. Spray sheet of foil with cooking spray. Cover baking dish with foil, sprayed side down.

3 Bake 1 hour. Uncover and bake 10 to 15 minutes longer or until juice of turkey is no longer pink when centers of thickest pieces are cut.

1 Serving: Calories 330 (Calories from Fat 60); Total Fat 7g (Saturated Fat 2.5g); Cholesterol 85mg; Sodium 620mg; Total Carbohydrate 37g (Dietary Fiber 3g); Protein 31g

Beef Stew

Prep Time: 15 min ▪ Start to Finish: 3 hrs 45 min ▪ 8 Servings (about 1¼ cups)

1 lb beef stew meat, cut into ½-inch pieces
1 medium onion, cut into eighths
1 bag (8 oz) baby-cut carrots (about 30)
1 can (14.5 oz) diced tomatoes, undrained
1 can (10½ oz) condensed beef broth
1 can (8 oz) tomato sauce
⅓ cup all-purpose flour
1 tablespoon Worcestershire sauce
1 teaspoon salt
1 teaspoon sugar
1 teaspoon dried marjoram leaves
¼ teaspoon pepper
12 small red potatoes (1½ lb), quartered
2 cups sliced fresh mushrooms (about 5 oz) or 1 package (3.4 oz) fresh shiitake
    mushrooms, sliced

1 Heat oven to 325°F.

2 In ovenproof 4-quart Dutch oven, mix all ingredients except potatoes and mushrooms. Cover and bake 2 hours, stirring once.

3 Stir in potatoes and mushrooms. Cover and bake 1 hour to 1 hour 30 minutes longer or until beef and vegetables are tender.

Slow Cooker Directions: Chop onion (½ cup). Omit tomato sauce. Increase flour to ½ cup. In 3½- to 6-quart slow cooker, mix all ingredients except beef. Add beef (do not stir). Cover and cook on low heat setting 8 to 9 hours. Stir well.

1 Serving: Calories 310 (Calories from Fat 60); Total Fat 7g (Saturated Fat 2.5g); Cholesterol 35mg; Sodium 820mg; Total Carbohydrate 43g (Dietary Fiber 6g); Protein 18g

Grilled Hamburgers with Roasted Sweet Onions

Prep Time: 25 min ▪ Start to Finish: 25 min ▪ 4 Servings

4 lean ground beef patties (4 to 6 oz each)
2 tablespoons steak sauce
1 package (1 oz) onion soup mix (from 2-oz box)
2 large sweet onions (Bermuda or other), cut in half, then thinly sliced
    and separated (6 cups)
2 tablespoons packed brown sugar
1 tablespoon balsamic vinegar

1 Heat gas or charcoal grill. Cut 2 (12×8-inch) sheets of heavy-duty foil; spray with cooking spray. Brush beef patties with steak sauce; sprinkle with half of the soup mix (dry).

2 Place half of the onions on center of each foil sheet. Sprinkle with remaining soup mix, brown sugar and vinegar. Bring up 2 sides of foil so edges meet. Seal edges, making tight ¹/₂-inch fold; fold again, allowing space for circulation and expansion. Fold other sides to seal.

3 Place packets and beef patties on grill. Cover grill; cook over medium heat 10 to 15 minutes, turning patties and rotating packets ¹/₂ turn once or twice, until meat thermometer inserted in center of patties reads 160°F. To serve onions, cut large X across top of each packet; carefully fold back foil to allow steam to escape. Serve onions with patties.

Go ahead and serve on buns, and add your favorite topping if
    you like.

1 Serving: Calories 320 (Calories from Fat 120); Total Fat 13g (Saturated Fat 5g); Cholesterol 70mg; Sodium 790mg; Total Carbohydrate 30g (Dietary Fiber 4g); Protein 22g

Caramelized-Onion Pot Roast

Prep Time: 25 min ▪ Start to Finish: 9 hrs 25 min ▪ 6 Servings

2$\frac{1}{2}$ lb beef boneless chuck roast
$\frac{1}{2}$ teaspoon salt
$\frac{1}{4}$ teaspoon pepper
1 tablespoon olive or vegetable oil
4 medium onions, sliced
1 cup beef broth
$\frac{1}{2}$ cup beer or apple juice
1 tablespoon packed brown sugar
1 tablespoon cider vinegar
2 tablespoons Dijon mustard
Horseradish, if desired

1 Spray 12-inch skillet with cooking spray; heat over medium-high heat. Cook beef in skillet 5 minutes, turning once, until brown. Season with salt and pepper; remove from skillet.

2 Reduce heat to medium. Add oil to skillet. Cook onions in oil 12 to 14 minutes, stirring frequently, until brown. Stir in broth, beer, brown sugar, vinegar and mustard. Spoon half of the onion mixture in 4- to 5-quart slow cooker. Place beef roast on onions. Spoon remaining onion mixture on beef.

3 Cover and cook on low heat setting 8 to 9 hours or until meat is tender.

4 Remove beef and onions from slow cooker and place on serving platter. Spoon some of the beef juices from slow cooker over beef. Serve with horseradish.

1 Serving: Calories 410 (Calories from Fat 215); Total Fat 24g (Saturated Fat 9g); Cholesterol 115mg; Sodium 530mg; Total Carbohydrate 10g (Dietary Fiber 2g); Protein 40g

In a hurry? Don't bother cooking the onions. Leave out the olive oil and mix the broth, beer, brown sugar, vinegar and mustard together. Place the onions in the slow cooker and top with beef and broth mixture.

Meat Loaf

Prep Time: 20 min ▪ Start to Finish: 1 hr 25 min ▪ 4 Servings

1 lb lean (at least 80%) ground beef
1 clove garlic, chopped
3 tablespoons chopped onion
2 slices bread with crust, torn into small pieces
$1/4$ cup milk
2 teaspoons Worcestershire sauce
1 teaspoon chopped fresh or $1/4$ teaspoon dried sage leaves
$1/4$ teaspoon salt
$1/4$ teaspoon ground mustard
$1/8$ teaspoon pepper
1 egg
$1/3$ cup ketchup, chili sauce or barbecue sauce

1 Heat the oven to 350°F. In a large bowl, break up the beef into small pieces, using a fork or spoon. Add the garlic, onion, bread, milk, Worcestershire sauce, sage, salt, mustard, pepper and egg. Mix with a fork, large spoon or your hands until the ingredients are well mixed.

2 Place the beef mixture in an ungreased 8-inch or 9-inch square pan and shape into an 8×4-inch loaf in the pan. Spread ketchup over the top.

3 Bake uncovered 50 to 60 minutes or until a meat thermometer inserted in the center of the loaf reads 160°F and center of loaf is no longer pink. Let the loaf stand 5 minutes.

Don't forget—leftover meatloaf makes satisfying, hearty sandwiches.

1 Serving: Calories 290 (Calories from Fat 130); Total Fat 15g (Saturated Fat 6g); Cholesterol 125mg; Sodium 560mg; Total Carbohydrate 15g (Dietary Fiber 0g); Protein 23g

Beef Stroganoff

Prep Time: 20 min ▪ Start to Finish: 50 min ▪ 6 Servings

1¹/₂ lb beef tenderloin or boneless top loin steak, about ¹/₂ inch thick

2 tablespoons butter or margarine

1¹/₂ cups beef broth

2 tablespoons ketchup

1 teaspoon salt

1 small clove garlic, finely chopped

3 cups sliced fresh mushrooms (8 oz)

1 medium onion, chopped (¹/₂ cup)

¹/₄ cup all-purpose flour

1 cup sour cream or plain yogurt

Hot cooked noodles or rice, if desired

1 Cut beef across grain into about 1¹/₂×¹/₂-inch strips. (Beef is easier to cut if partially frozen, 30 to 60 minutes.) In 12-inch skillet, melt butter over medium-high heat. Cook beef in butter, stirring occasionally, until brown.

2 Reserve ¹/₃ cup of the broth. Stir remaining broth, the ketchup, salt and garlic into beef. Heat to boiling; reduce heat. Cover and simmer about 10 minutes or until beef is tender. Stir in mushrooms and onion. Heat to boiling; reduce heat. Cover and simmer about 5 minutes or until onion is tender.

3 In tightly covered container, shake reserved ¹/₃ cup broth and the flour until mixed; gradually stir into beef mixture. Heat to boiling, stirring constantly. Boil and stir 1 minute; reduce heat to low.

4 Stir in sour cream; heat until hot. Serve over noodles.

Mix up your mushrooms! Instead of traditional white or button mushrooms, combine several fresh varieties such as baby portabella, shiitake and oyster mushrooms.

1 Serving: Calories 330 (Calories from Fat 180); Total Fat 20g (Saturated Fat 10g); Cholesterol 100mg; Sodium 810mg; Total Carbohydrate 10g (Dietary Fiber 1g); Protein 28g

Mama's Spaghetti and Meatballs

Prep Time: 25 min ■ Start to Finish: 1 hr 20 min ■ 4 Servings

Spaghetti and Sauce
2 tablespoons olive oil
1 large onion, chopped (1 cup)
1 small green bell pepper, chopped (1/2 cup)
2 large cloves garlic, finely chopped
2 cans (14 1/2 oz each) whole tomatoes, undrained
2 cans (8 oz each) tomato sauce
2 tablespoons chopped fresh or 2 teaspoons dried basil leaves
1 tablespoon chopped fresh or 1 teaspoon dried oregano leaves
1/2 teaspoon salt
1/2 teaspoon fennel seed
1/4 teaspoon pepper
Hot cooked spaghetti

Meatballs
1 lb ground chuck or lean ground beef
1/2 cup unseasoned dry bread crumbs
1/2 cup buttermilk
1/2 teaspoon salt
1/2 teaspoon Worcestershire sauce
1/4 teaspoon pepper
1 small onion, chopped (1/4 cup)
1 egg

1 In 3-quart saucepan, heat oil over medium heat. Cook 1 cup onion, the bell pepper and garlic in oil 2 minutes, stirring occasionally, till soft but not brown. Stir in remaining sauce ingredients, breaking up tomatoes with a fork. Heat to boiling; reduce heat. Cover and simmer 45 minutes. Stir occasionally.

2 Meanwhile, heat oven to 400°F. In large bowl, mix all meatball ingredients. Shape mixture into twenty 1 1/2-inch meatballs. (Wet your hands to shape, or use a small ice cream scoop.) Place in ungreased 13×9-inch pan.

3 Bake meatballs uncovered 20 to 25 minutes or until thoroughly cooked and no longer pink in center. Serve hot cooked spaghetti with sauce and meatballs.

1 Serving: Calories 680 (Calories from Fat 210); Total Fat 24g (Saturated Fat 7g); Cholesterol 125mg; Sodium 1780mg; Total Carbohydrate 80g (Dietary Fiber 9g); Protein 36g

Classic Chili

Prep Time: 15 min ▪ Start to Finish: 1 hr 40 min ▪ 4 Servings

1 lb lean ground (at least 8%) beef
1 medium onion, chopped (¹/₂ cup)
1 clove garlic, finely chopped
1 can (14¹/₂ oz) diced tomatoes, undrained
1 can (8 oz) tomato sauce
1 tablespoon chili powder
³/₄ teaspoon ground cumin
¹/₄ teaspoon salt
¹/₄ teaspoon pepper
1 can (15 or 16 oz) kidney or pinto beans, drained and rinsed, if desired

1 Cook beef, onion and garlic in 3-quart saucepan over medium heat 8 to 10 minutes, stirring occasionally, until beef is brown; drain.

2 Stir in remaining ingredients except beans. Heat to boiling; reduce heat to low. Cover and simmer 1 hour, stirring occasionally.

3 Stir in beans. Heat to boiling; reduce heat to low. Simmer uncovered about 10 minutes, stirring occasionally, until desired thickness.

Want to turn up the heat? Increase the chili powder, add ¹/₂ teaspoon red pepper sauce or add a jalapeño chili, seeded and finely chopped, to the mix.

1 Serving: Calories 395 (Calories from Fat 155); Total Fat 17g (Saturated Fat 7g); Cholesterol 65mg; Sodium 970mg; Total Carbohydrate 37g (Dietary Fiber 10g); Protein 33g

Grandma's Macaroni and Cheese

Prep Time: 25 min ▪ Start to Finish: 50 min ▪ 4 Servings

2 cups uncooked elbow macaroni (7 oz)
1/4 cup butter
1/4 cup all-purpose flour
1/2 teaspoon salt
1/4 teaspoon pepper
1/4 teaspoon ground mustard
1/4 teaspoon Worcestershire sauce
2 cups milk
2 cups shredded sharp Cheddar cheese (8 oz)

1 Heat oven to 350°F. Cook and drain macaroni as directed on package.

2 Meanwhile, in 3-quart saucepan, melt butter over low heat. Stir in flour, 1/2 teaspoon salt, the pepper, mustard and Worcestershire sauce. Cook over low heat, stirring constantly, until mixture is smooth and bubbly; remove from heat. Stir in milk. Heat to boiling, stirring constantly. Boil and stir 1 minute; remove from heat. Stir in cheese until melted.

3 Gently stir macaroni into cheese sauce. Pour into ungreased 2-quart casserole.

4 Bake uncovered 20 to 25 minutes or until bubbly.

1 Serving: Calories 610 (Calories from Fat 300); Total Fat 34g (Saturated Fat 19g); Cholesterol 100mg; Sodium 790mg; Total Carbohydrate 51g (Dietary Fiber 3g); Protein 26g

Add surprise to your mac 'n' cheese—mix up your cheeses! Try Jarlsberg, smoked Gouda or white Cheddar for all or half of the sharp Cheddar.

Baked Potato Bar

Prep Time: 10 min ▪ Start to Finish: 8 hrs 10 min ▪ 12 Servings

12 unpeeled russet potatoes (6 to 8 oz each)
2 tablespoons olive or vegetable oil
1¹/₂ teaspoons salt
1 teaspoon coarse black pepper
Assorted toppings (such as sour cream, ranch dip, chopped bell pepper,
    bacon bits, assorted shredded cheeses, crumbled blue cheese,
    chopped green onions, salsa), if desired

1 Pierce potatoes with fork. Place potatoes and oil in large plastic food-storage bag; toss to coat with oil. Sprinkle with salt and pepper. Wrap potatoes individually in aluminum foil; place in 5- to 6-quart slow cooker.

2 Cover and cook on low heat setting 6 to 8 hours or until potatoes are tender. Serve with toppings.

1 Serving: Calories 160 (Calories from Fat 20); Total Fat 1g (Saturated Fat 0g); Cholesterol 0mg; Sodium 310mg; Total Carbohydrate 35g (Dietary Fiber 3g); Protein 3g

Down-Home Mashed Potatoes

Prep Time: 10 min ▪ Start to Finish: 40 min ▪ 4 to 6 Servings

6 medium round red or white potatoes (2 lb)
$1/3$ to $1/2$ cup milk, half-and-half or whipping cream
$1/4$ cup butter, softened
$1/2$ teaspoon salt
Dash of pepper
Chopped fresh parsley or chives, if desired

1 In 2-quart saucepan, place potatoes and enough water just to cover potatoes. Heat to boiling; reduce heat. Cover and simmer 20 to 30 minutes or until potatoes are tender; drain. Shake pan with potatoes over low heat to dry (this will help mashed potatoes be fluffier).

2 Mash potatoes in pan with potato masher until no lumps remain. Add milk in small amounts, mashing after each addition (the amount needed depends on kind of potatoes used).

3 Add butter, salt and pepper. Mash vigorously until potatoes are light and fluffy. If desired, sprinkle with small pieces of butter or sprinkle with paprika, chopped fresh parsley or chives.

1 Serving: Calories 270 (Calories from Fat 110); Total Fat 12g (Saturated Fat 6g); Cholesterol 30mg; Sodium 390mg; Total Carbohydrate 38g (Dietary Fiber 4g); Protein 4g

Applesauce

Prep Time: 5 min ▪ Start to Finish: 20 min ▪ 6 Servings (about 1 cup)

4 medium cooking apples (1⅓ lb), peeled, quartered and cored
½ cup water
¼ cup packed brown sugar or 3 to 4 tablespoons granulated sugar
¼ teaspoon ground cinnamon
⅛ teaspoon ground nutmeg

1 In 2-quart saucepan, heat apples and water to boiling over medium heat, stirring occasionally; reduce heat. Simmer uncovered 5 to 10 minutes, stirring occasionally to break up apples, until tender.

2 Stir in remaining ingredients. Heat to boiling. Boil and stir 1 minute. Cover and refrigerate until serving. Store covered in refrigerator.

Slow Cooker Directions: Decrease the water to ¼ cup. In a 3½- to 6-quart slow cooker, mix all ingredients. Cover and cook on high heat setting 1 hour 30 minutes to 2 hours or until apples are tender; stir.

1 Serving: Calories 90 (Calories from Fat 0); Total Fat 0g (Saturated Fat 0g); Cholesterol 0mg; Sodium 5mg; Total Carbohydrate 22g (Dietary Fiber 2g); Protein 0g

Old-Fashioned Baked Beans

Prep Time: 20 min ▪ Start to Finish: 6 hrs 35 min ▪ 10 Servings (about ½ cup)

2 cups dried navy beans (1 lb),
   sorted, rinsed
10 cups water
½ cup packed brown sugar
½ cup molasses

1 teaspoon salt
6 slices bacon, crisply cooked and
   crumbled (about ⅓ cup)
1 medium onion, chopped (½ cup)
3 cups water

1 Heat oven to 350°F.

2 In ovenproof 4-quart Dutch oven, heat beans and 10 cups water to boiling. Boil uncovered 2 minutes. Stir in remaining ingredients except 3 cups water.

3 Cover and bake 4 hours, stirring occasionally.

4 Stir in 3 cups water. Bake uncovered 2 hours to 2 hours 15 minutes longer, stirring occasionally, until beans are tender and desired consistency.

Slow Cooker Directions: In 3½- to 6-quart slow cooker, place beans and 5 cups water. Cover and cook on high heat setting 2 hours. Turn off heat; let stand 8 to 24 hours. Stir in brown sugar, molasses, salt, bacon and onion. Cover and cook on low heat setting 10 to 12 hours or until beans are very tender and most of liquid is absorbed.

These beans are great with coleslaw – buy a bagged mix at the store and mix it up in a minute.

1 Serving: Calories 240 (Calories from Fat 25); Total Fat 3g (Saturated Fat 1g); Cholesterol 0mg; Sodium 320mg; Total Carbohydrate 43g (Dietary Fiber 6g); Protein 10g

Red Beans and Rice

Prep Time: 10 min   ▪   Start to Finish: 9 hrs 10 min   ▪   8 Servings (1 ¼ cups each)

2 smoked pork hocks (about 1¼ lb)
1 small onion, chopped (¼ cup)
1 can (15 oz) red beans, drained,
   rinsed
1 dried bay leaf
1 can (15 oz) tomato sauce
1 tablespoon red pepper sauce
1 medium bell pepper, coarsely
   chopped (¾ cup)

3 cups water
3 cups uncooked instant rice
2 teaspoons Cajun seasoning
1 lb fully cooked smoked sausage,
   cut lengthwise in half, then cut
   crosswise into 1-inch pieces

1 Place pork hocks in 3- to 4-quart slow cooker. Top with onion, beans, bay leaf, tomato sauce, pepper sauce and bell pepper in order listed.

2 Cover and cook on low heat setting 8 to 9 hours.

3 About 30 minutes before serving, heat water to boiling in 2-quart saucepan over high heat. Remove from heat and stir in rice. Cover and let stand about 5 minutes or until water is absorbed. Fluff rice with fork before serving.

4 Meanwhile, remove pork from cooker; place on cutting board. Pull meat from bones, using 2 forks; discard bones and skin. Return pork to cooker. Stir in Cajun seasoning and sausage. Increase heat setting to high. Cover and cook 15 minutes or until sausage is heated through.

5 For each serving, place ½ cup rice in soup bowl and top with ¾ cup red bean mixture.

If you can't find smoked pork hocks, just use 1 cup cubed fully cooked ham.

1 Serving: Calories 475 (Calories from Fat 190); Total Fat 21g (Saturated Fat 7g); Cholesterol 55mg; Sodium 1420mg; Total Carbohydrate 54g (Dietary Fiber 5g); Protein 22g

Wake Up to Fresh Bread

Apricot Breakfast Bread

Prep Time: 25 min
Start to Finish: 2 hrs 25 min
1 Loaf (16 slices)

1 cup all-purpose flour	1 cup buttermilk
3/4 cup whole wheat flour	2 tablespoons canola oil
3/4 cup packed brown sugar	1/2 cup chopped dried apricots
1 teaspoon baking soda	1/3 cup chopped walnuts
1 teaspoon ground cinnamon	1 tablespoon granulated sugar
1/4 teaspoon salt	1/2 teaspoon ground cinnamon
1 egg or 2 egg whites	

1.   Heat oven to 350°F (or 325°F if using dark or nonstick pan). Grease bottom and sides of 8×4- or 9×5-inch loaf pan with shortening or cooking spray; coat with flour.

2.   In medium bowl, mix flours, brown sugar, baking soda, 1 teaspoon cinnamon and the salt; set aside. In another medium bowl, stir egg, buttermilk and oil until well blended. Add to flour mixture and stir just until moistened (some lumps will remain). Stir in apricots and walnuts. Spread in pan.

3.   In small bowl, mix granulated sugar and 1/2 teaspoon cinnamon; sprinkle evenly over batter in pan.

4.   Bake 50 to 60 minutes or until golden brown and toothpick inserted in center comes out clean. Cool 10 minutes; unmold onto wire rack and cool completely. When completely cool, wrap in plastic wrap. Best served the next day.

1 Slice: Calories 150 (Calories from Fat 35); Total Fat 4 (Saturated Fat 0g); Cholesterol 15mg; Sodium 140mg; Total Carbohydrate 25g (Dietary Fiber 2g); Protein 3g

Make this quick bread the day ahead to have a breakfast treat waiting for you. Add a newspaper and coffee and you've got the perfect lazy weekend morning.

Easy Cheese Casserole Bread

Prep Time: 10 min
Start to Finish: 2 hrs 25 min
1 Loaf (24 slices)

1 package regular or quick active dry yeast (2 ¼ teaspoons)
½ cup warm water (105°F to 115°F)
½ cup lukewarm milk (scalded then cooled)
⅔ cup butter or margarine, softened
2 eggs
1 teaspoon salt
3 cups all-purpose flour
1 cup shredded Swiss or Cheddar cheese (4 oz)
½ teaspoon pepper
Additional butter or margarine, softened

1.   In large bowl, dissolve yeast in warm water. Add milk, ⅔ cup butter, the eggs, salt and 1 cup of the flour. Beat with electric mixer on low speed 30 seconds, scraping bowl constantly. Beat on medium speed 2 minutes, scraping bowl occasionally. Stir in remaining flour, the cheese and pepper. Scrape batter from side of bowl.

2.   Cover and let rise in warm place about 40 minutes or until doubled in size. Batter is ready if indentation remains when touched with floured finger.

3.   Grease bottom and side of 2-quart casserole. Stir down batter by beating about 25 strokes. Spread evenly in casserole. Cover and let rise about 45 minutes or until doubled in size.

4.   Move oven rack to low position so that top of casserole will be in center of oven. Heat oven to 375°F. Bake 40 to 45 minutes or until loaf is brown and sounds hollow when tapped. Loosen side of bread from casserole; immediately remove from casserole to wire rack. Brush top of bread with additional butter; cool.

1 Slice: Calories 130 (Calories from Fat 70); Total Fat 7g (Saturated Fat 3.5g); Cholesterol 35mg; Sodium 150mg; Total Carbohydrate 12g (Dietary Fiber 0g); Protein 4g

No kneading! Batter breads like this take less time to make than most breads, but you still get the homey smell and wonderful taste.

Raspberry-Banana Yogurt Smoothies

Creamy Mango Smoothies

Sour Cream–Honey Fruit Salad

Mediterranean Quinoa Salad

Summer Chicken-Potato Salad

Middle East Vegetable Tacos

Five-Spice Tofu Stir-Fry

Vegetarian Chili with Spicy Tortilla Strips

Winter Vegetable Stew

Shrimp Kabobs and Warm Spinach Salad

Salmon with Ginger-Citrus Salsa

Lemony Fish over Vegetables and Rice

Garden Ratatouille

Sesame-Garlic Broccoli

Herb-Roasted Root Vegetables

3

good for you

Raspberry-Banana Yogurt Smoothies

Prep Time: 5 min ▪ Start to Finish: 5 min ▪ 2 Servings (about 1¹/₂ cups each)

1 container (6 oz) 99% fat-free French vanilla yogurt
1¹/₂ cups soymilk
1 cup frozen or fresh unsweetened raspberries
1 medium banana, sliced (1 cup)

1 Place all ingredients in blender or food processor. Cover; blend on high speed about 30 seconds or until smooth.

2 Pour into 2 glasses. Serve immediately.

1 Serving: Calories 290 (Calories from Fat 35); Total Fat 4g (Saturated Fat 1g); Cholesterol 5mg; Sodium 160mg; Total Carbohydrate 54g (Dietary Fiber 10g); Protein 9g

Creamy Mango Smoothies

Prep Time: 10 min ▪ Start to Finish: 10 min ▪ 6 Servings (1 cup each)

2 mangoes, seed removed, peeled and chopped (2 cups)
2 cups mango sorbet
2 containers (6 oz each) French vanilla low-fat yogurt
1¹/₂ cups fat-free (skim) milk or soymilk

In blender, place all ingredients. Cover; blend on high speed until smooth.

Get the best flavor and color with ripe mangoes. Look for
skins that are yellow with blushes of red.

1 Serving: Calories 200 (Calories from Fat 10); Total Fat 1g (Saturated Fat 0.5g); Cholesterol 0mg;
Sodium 75mg; Total Carbohydrate 43g (Dietary Fiber 1g); Protein 5g

Sour Cream–Honey Fruit Salad

Prep Time: 15 min ▪ Start to Finish: 15 min ▪ 10 Servings

1/2 cup sour cream
1 tablespoon honey
1 tablespoon orange juice
4 medium oranges, peeled and sectioned
3 medium bananas, sliced
1 cup halved fresh strawberries
1 cup halved seedless green grapes

1 In large bowl, mix sour cream, honey and orange juice until smooth.

2 Add oranges, bananas, strawberries and grapes; toss gently to mix.

1 Serving: Calories 105 (Calories from Fat 25); Total Fat 3g (Saturated Fat 1g); Cholesterol 5mg; Sodium 5mg; Total Carbohydrate 21g (Dietary Fiber 3g); Protein 1g

Mediterranean Quinoa Salad

Prep Time: 30 min ▪ Start to Finish: 1 hr 35 min ▪ 4 Servings (³/₄ cup each)

1 cup uncooked quinoa
2 cups reduced-sodium chicken broth
¹/₂ cup chopped drained roasted red bell peppers (from 7-oz jar)
¹/₂ cup cubed provolone cheese
¹/₄ cup chopped kalamata olives
2 tablespoons chopped fresh basil leaves
1 teaspoon roasted garlic (from 4-oz jar)
2 tablespoons fat-free Italian dressing

1 Rinse quinoa under cold water 1 minute; drain.

2 In 2-quart saucepan, heat quinoa and broth to boiling; reduce heat. Cover; simmer 15 to 20 minutes or until quinoa is tender; drain. Cool completely, about 45 minutes.

3 In large serving bowl, toss quinoa and remaining ingredients. Serve immediately, or refrigerate 1 to 2 hours before serving.

Don't skip rinsing the quinoa—it has a bitter coating. Then, it's completely delicious!

1 Serving: Calories 250 (Calories from Fat 70); Total Fat 8g (Saturated Fat 3g); Cholesterol 10mg; Sodium 590mg; Total Carbohydrate 33g (Dietary Fiber 3g); Protein 12g

Summer Chicken-Potato Salad

Prep Time: 15 min ▮ Start to Finish: 35 min ▮ 4 Servings

4 medium red potatoes (1 lb), cut into ³/₄-inch cubes
¹/₂ lb fresh green beans, trimmed, cut into 1-inch pieces (about 2 cups)
¹/₂ cup fat-free plain yogurt
¹/₃ cup fat-free ranch dressing
1 tablespoon prepared horseradish
¹/₄ teaspoon salt
Dash of pepper
2 cups cut-up cooked chicken breast
²/₃ cup thinly sliced celery
Torn salad greens, if desired

1 Heat 6 cups lightly salted water to boiling in 2-quart saucepan. Add potatoes; return to boiling. Reduce heat; simmer 5 minutes. Add green beans; cook uncovered 8 to 12 minutes longer or until potatoes and beans are crisp-tender.

2 Meanwhile, mix yogurt, dressing, horseradish, salt and pepper in small bowl; set aside.

3 Drain potatoes and green beans; rinse with cold water to cool. Mix potatoes, green beans, chicken and celery in large serving bowl. Pour yogurt mixture over salad; toss gently to coat. Line plates with greens; spoon salad onto greens.

1 Serving: Calories 280 (Calories from Fat 35); Total Fat 3.5g (Saturated Fat 1g); Cholesterol 60mg; Sodium 410mg; Total Carbohydrate 37g (Dietary Fiber 5g); Protein 26g

Middle East Vegetable Tacos

Prep Time: 10 min ■ Start to Finish: 22 min ■ 6 Servings

1 tablespoon olive or vegetable oil
1 medium eggplant (1 lb), peeled and cut into 1/2-inch cubes
1 medium red bell pepper, cut into 1/2-inch strips
1 medium onion, cut into 1/2-inch wedges
1 can (14.5 oz) diced tomatoes with roasted garlic, onion and oregano
    (or other variety), undrained
1/4 teaspoon salt
1 container (8 oz) refrigerated hummus
12 taco shells
Plain yogurt or sour cream, if desired

1 In 10-inch nonstick skillet, heat oil over medium-high heat. Cook eggplant, bell pepper and onion in oil 5 to 7 minutes, stirring occasionally, until vegetables are crisp-tender.

2 Stir in tomatoes and salt; reduce heat to medium. Cover and cook about 5 minutes or until eggplant is tender.

3 Spread slightly less than 2 tablespoons hummus on half of inside of each taco shell. Spoon about 1/2 cup vegetable mixture over hummus in each shell. Serve with yogurt.

This vegetable mixture also tastes great served over pasta.

1 Serving: Calories 280 (Calories from Fat 110); Total Fat 12g (Saturated Fat 1.5g); Cholesterol 0mg; Sodium 440mg; Total Carbohydrate 37g (Dietary Fiber 8g); Protein 7g

Five-Spice Tofu Stir-Fry

Prep Time: 40 min ▪ Start to Finish: 50 min ▪ 4 Servings

1 cup uncooked instant brown rice
1/4 cup stir-fry sauce
2 tablespoons orange juice
1 tablespoon honey
3/3 teaspoon five-spice powder
1 package (14 oz) firm tofu,
    cut into 3/4-inch cubes

1 small red onion, cut into thin
    wedges
1 bag (1 lb) frozen baby bean
    and carrot blend
1/4 cup water

1 Cook rice according to the directions on the package.

2 Meanwhile, mix stir-fry sauce, orange juice, honey and five-spice powder in medium bowl. Press tofu between paper towels to absorb excess moisture. Stir tofu into sauce mixture; let marinate 10 minutes.

3 Spray 12-inch nonstick skillet with cooking spray; heat over medium heat. Remove tofu from sauce mixture; reserve sauce mixture. Cook tofu in skillet 3 to 4 minutes, stirring occasionally, just until light golden brown. Remove tofu from skillet.

4 Cook onion in skillet 2 minutes, stirring constantly. Add frozen vegetables and 1/4 cup water. Heat to boiling; reduce heat to medium. Cover and cook 6 to 8 minutes, stirring occasionally, until vegetables are crisp-tender.

5 Stir in reserved sauce mixture and tofu. Cook 2 to 3 minutes, stirring occasionally, until mixture is slightly thickened and hot. Serve over rice.

The 5-spice powder adds terrific Chinese flavor—look for it in the spice section of your supermarket.

1 Serving: Calories 290 (Calories from Fat 60); Total Fat 7g (Saturated Fat 1g); Cholesterol 0mg; Sodium 580mg; Total Carbohydrate 43g (Dietary Fiber 7g); Protein 15g

Vegetarian Chili with Spicy Tortilla Strips

Prep Time: 10 min ▪ Start to Finish: 6 hrs 22 min ▪ 6 Servings

Spicy Tortilla Strips
3 corn tortillas (6 inches in diameter)
1 tablespoon vegetable oil
Dash of ground red pepper (cayenne)

Chili
1 can (15 to 16 oz) dark red kidney beans, drained
1 can (15 to 16 oz) spicy chili beans, undrained
1 can (15 oz) pinquito beans, undrained
1 can (14$^1/_2$ oz) chili-style chunky tomatoes, undrained
1 large onion, chopped (1 cup)
2 to 3 teaspoons chili powder
$^1/_8$ teaspoon ground red pepper (cayenne)

1 To make tortilla strips, heat oven to 375°F. Brush both sides of tortillas with oil. Lightly sprinkle red pepper on one side of tortillas. Cut into $^1/_2$-inch strips. Place in single layer on ungreased cookie sheet. Bake 10 to 12 minutes or until strips are crisp and edges are light brown.

2 To make chili, mix ingredients in 3$^1/_2$- to 4-quart slow cooker.

3 Cover and cook on low heat setting 5 to 6 hours or until flavors have blended. Stir well before serving. Top each serving with tortilla strips.

1 Serving: Calories 255 (Calories from Fat 10); Total Fat 1g (Saturated Fat 0g); Cholesterol 0mg; Sodium 1010mg; Total Carbohydrate 59g (Dietary Fiber 15g); Protein 17g

Pinquitos are small, tender, pink beans. If you have difficulty locating them at your supermarket, just substitute pinto beans.

Winter Vegetable Stew

Prep Time: 20 min ■ Start to Finish: 10 hrs 40 min ■ 8 Servings

1 can (28 oz) Italian-style peeled whole tomatoes
4 medium red potatoes, cut into 1/2-inch pieces
4 medium stalks celery, cut into 1/2-inch pieces (2 cups)
3 medium carrots, cut into 1/2-inch pieces (11/2 cups)
2 medium parsnips, peeled and cut into 1/2-inch pieces
2 medium leeks, cut into 1/2-inch pieces
1 can (14 oz) chicken broth
1/2 teaspoon dried thyme leaves
1/2 teaspoon dried rosemary leaves
1/2 teaspoon salt
3 tablespoons cornstarch
3 tablespoons cold water

1 Drain tomatoes, reserving liquid. Cut up tomatoes. In 4- to 5-quart slow cooker, mix tomatoes, tomato liquid and remaining ingredients except cornstarch and water.

2 Cover and cook on low heat setting 8 to 10 hours.

3 In small bowl, mix cornstarch and water; gradually stir into stew until blended. Increase heat setting to high. Cover and cook about 20 minutes, stirring occasionally, until thickened.

1 Serving: Calories 150 (Calories from Fat 5); Total Fat 0.5g (Saturated Fat 0g); Cholesterol 0mg; Sodium 550mg; Total Carbohydrate 31g (Dietary Fiber 5g); Protein 4g

Shrimp Kabobs and Warm Spinach Salad

Prep Time: 20 min ▪ Start to Finish: 50 min ▪ 4 Servings

Kabobs

8 wooden skewers (8 to 10 inch),
    soaked in water 30 minutes
¼ cup dry white wine or chicken broth
2 teaspoons olive oil
1 teaspoon grated lemon peel
2 tablespoons lemon juice
3 cloves garlic, finely chopped
1 tablespoon chopped fresh or 1 teaspoon
    dried basil leaves
1 lb uncooked deveined peeled large shrimp
    (21 to 30), thawed if frozen, tail shells removed

Salad

6 cups spinach leaves
2 plum (Roma) tomatoes,
    chopped (⅔ cup)
2 tablespoons chopped onion
3 tablespoons fat-free balsamic
    vinaigrette

1 In shallow glass or plastic dish, mix wine, oil, lemon peel, lemon juice, garlic and basil. Add shrimp, turning to coat with marinade. Cover and refrigerate at least 30 minutes but no longer than 2 hours to marinate.

2 Prepare gas or charcoal grill for medium heat. Remove shrimp from marinade; reserve marinade. Thread shrimp on skewers, leaving space between each.

3 Grill kabobs, covered, 3 to 5 minutes, turning and brushing 2 or 3 times with marinade, until shrimp are pink.

4 In large bowl, toss salad ingredients. On serving plate, place spinach salad; top with shrimp kabobs.

1 Serving: Calories 130 (Calories from Fat 30); Total Fat 3.5g (Saturated Fat 0.5g); Cholesterol 160mg; Sodium 400mg; Total Carbohydrate 6g (Dietary Fiber 2g); Protein 19g

Salmon with Ginger-Citrus Salsa

Prep Time: 30 min ▪ Start to Finish: 2 hrs 40 min ▪ 4 Servings

Salmon	Salsa
1 lemon	2 navel oranges, peeled, finely chopped
4 cups water	1 lime, peeled, finely chopped
6 thin slices gingerroot	1/2 cup chopped red bell pepper
1/2 teaspoon salt	2 tablespoons chopped fresh chives
1/4 teaspoon coarsely ground pepper	1 tablespoon honey
1 lb salmon fillets, cut into 4 pieces	1 teaspoon grated gingerroot
	1 teaspoon olive oil

1 Grate enough peel from lemon to make 2 teaspoons; set aside for salsa. Cut lemon into slices. In 10- or 12-inch skillet, heat lemon slices, water, sliced gingerroot, salt and pepper to boiling. Boil 3 minutes; reduce heat to medium-low.

2 Add salmon, skin side down, to skillet. Cover and cook 7 to 10 minutes or until salmon flakes easily with fork. Carefully remove salmon with slotted spoon; place in baking dish. Cover; refrigerate at least 2 hours but no longer than 24 hours. Discard liquid mixture in skillet.

3 In medium glass or plastic bowl, mix oranges, lime, bell pepper, chives, honey, grated gingerroot, oil and reserved 2 teaspoons lemon peel.

4 To serve, carefully remove skin from salmon; place salmon on serving plate. Spoon salsa over salmon, using slotted spoon.

This is a good do-ahead recipe—you can make the fish up to 24 hours before serving.

1 Serving: Calories 240 (Calories from Fat 70); Total Fat 8g (Saturated Fat 2g); Cholesterol 75mg; Sodium 370mg; Total Carbohydrate 17g (Dietary Fiber 3g); Protein 25g

Lemony Fish over Vegetables and Rice

Prep Time: 30 min ▪ Start to Finish: 30 min ▪ 4 Servings

1 box (6 oz) fried rice (rice and vermicelli mix with almonds and Oriental
 seasonings)
2 tablespoons butter or margarine
2 cups water
$1/2$ teaspoon grated lemon peel
1 bag (1 lb) frozen broccoli, corn and peppers (or other combination)
1 lb cod, haddock or other mild-flavored fish fillets, about $1/2$ inch thick, cut into
 4 serving pieces
$1/2$ teaspoon lemon-pepper seasoning
1 tablespoon lemon juice
Chopped fresh parsley, if desired

1 In 12-inch nonstick skillet, cook rice and butter over medium heat about 3 minutes, stirring occasionally, until rice is golden brown. Stir in water, seasoning packet from rice mix and lemon peel. Heat to boiling; reduce heat to low. Cover; simmer 10 minutes.

2 Stir in frozen vegetables. Heat to boiling over medium-high heat, stirring occasionally. Arrange fish on rice mixture. Sprinkle fish with lemon-pepper seasoning; drizzle with lemon juice.

3 Reduce heat to low. Cover; simmer 8 to 12 minutes or until fish flakes easily with fork and vegetables are tender. Sprinkle with parsley.

1 Serving: Calories 250 (Calories from Fat 70); Total Fat 8g (Saturated Fat 4g); Cholesterol 75mg; Sodium 620mg; Total Carbohydrate 19g (Dietary Fiber 3g); Protein 26g

Garden Ratatouille

Prep Time: 25 min ▪ Start to Finish: 25 min ▪ 8 Servings

3 cups $1/2$-inch cubes eggplant (1 lb)
1 small zucchini, cut into $1/4$-inch slices (1 cup)
1 small onion, sliced
$1/2$ medium green bell pepper, cut into strips
2 cloves garlic, finely chopped
2 tablespoons chopped fresh parsley
1 tablespoon chopped fresh or $1/2$ teaspoon dried basil leaves
2 tablespoons water
$1/2$ teaspoon salt
$1/4$ teaspoon pepper
2 medium very ripe tomatoes, cut into eighths

1 In 10-inch skillet, cook all ingredients except tomatoes over medium heat about 10 minutes, stirring occasionally, until vegetables are tender; remove from heat.

2 Stir in tomatoes. (For added flavor, drizzle with about 2 tablespoons olive oil, if desired.) Cover and let stand 2 to 3 minutes until tomatoes are warm.

This is a great summer recipe, though you can feel free to make it any time of year.

1 Serving: Calories 25 (Calories from Fat 0); Total Fat 0g (Saturated Fat 0g); Cholesterol 0mg; Sodium 150mg; Total Carbohydrate 5g (Dietary Fiber 2g); Protein 0g

Sesame-Garlic Broccoli

Prep Time: 20 min ▪ Start to Finish: 40 min ▪ 4 Servings (½ cup each)

2 cups broccoli florets (¾ lb)	3 tablespoons vegetable oil
¼ cup chicken broth	¼ teaspoon dark sesame oil, if desired
2 tablespoons rice wine or chicken broth	1 tablespoon finely chopped garlic
1 teaspoon cornstarch	2 teaspoons grated gingerroot
1 teaspoon packed brown sugar	1 tablespoon sesame seed, toasted

1 In 10-inch skillet, heat 1 inch water to boiling. Add broccoli and boil uncovered 3 to 5 minutes or until just tender. Drain broccoli and immediately rinse under cold water to stop cooking. Set broccoli aside.

2 In small bowl, mix broth, rice wine, cornstarch and brown sugar until smooth.

3 In same skillet, heat vegetable oil and sesame oil over medium heat until oils shimmer. Add broccoli and cook about 1 minute, stirring frequently. Add garlic and gingerroot and cook 1 minute longer; do not let garlic burn.

4 Stir cornstarch mixture again to dissolve any lumps and add to skillet. Heat mixture to boiling, stirring constantly. Cook and stir 1 minute longer. Remove from heat and sprinkle with toasted sesame seed.

To toast sesame seed, heat seeds in a skillet over medium-low heat 5 to 7 minutes, stirring frequently, until browning begins. Then stir constantly until seeds are golden brown. Immediately remove seeds from skillet and set aside.

1 Serving: Calories 130 (Calories from Fat 110); Total Fat 12g (Saturated Fat 1.5g); Cholesterol 0mg; Sodium 105mg; Total Carbohydrate 5g (Dietary Fiber 2g); Protein 2g

Herb-Roasted Root Vegetables

Prep Time: 15 min ▪ Start to Finish: 1 hr 10 min ▪ 6 Servings (¹/₂ cup each)

2 medium turnips, peeled, cut into 1-inch pieces (3 cups)
2 medium parsnips, peeled, cut into ¹/₂-inch pieces (1¹/₂ cups)
1 medium red onion, cut into 1-inch wedges (1 cup)
1 cup ready-to-eat baby-cut carrots
Cooking spray
2 teaspoons Italian seasoning
¹/₂ teaspoon coarse salt

1 Heat oven to 425°F. Spray 15×10×1-inch pan with cooking spray. Arrange vegetables in single layer in pan. Spray with cooking spray (2 or 3 seconds). Sprinkle with Italian seasoning and salt.

2 Roast uncovered 45 to 55 minutes, stirring once, until vegetables are tender.

1 Serving: Calories 70 (Calories from Fat 0); Total Fat 0.5g (Saturated Fat 0g); Cholesterol 0mg; Sodium 230mg; Total Carbohydrate 14g (Dietary Fiber 4g); Protein 1g

Lasagna Primavera

Spinach Gnocchi with Nutmeg

Shrimp Creole

Cioppino (Italian Seafood Stew)

Bayou Gumbo

Chicken Penne with Vodka Sauce

Chile-Chicken Tacos

Picadillo Chicken Paella

Southern Turkey and Lentil Casserole

Jamaican Jerk Pork Chops with Mango Salsa

Slow-Cooked Pork Burrito Bowls

Provençal Pork Roast

Barbecued Ribs

Beef Tagine

Curried Coconut Beef with Winter Vegetables

comforting ethnic foods

4

Lasagna Primavera

Prep Time: 20 min ■ Start to Finish: 1 hr 35 min ■ 8 Servings

12 uncooked lasagna noodles
3 cups frozen broccoli florets (from 14-oz bag), thawed, well drained, cut into
    bite-sized pieces
3 large carrots, coarsely shredded (2 cups)
1 can (14.5 oz) diced tomatoes, well drained
2 medium bell peppers, cut into $^1/_2$-inch pieces
1 container (15 oz) ricotta cheese
$^1/_2$ cup grated Parmesan cheese
1 egg
2 containers (10 oz each) refrigerated Alfredo sauce
2 bags (8 oz each) shredded mozzarella cheese (4 cups)

1 Cook and drain noodles as directed on package.

2 In large bowl, mix broccoli, carrots, tomatoes and bell peppers. In small bowl, mix ricotta cheese, Parmesan cheese, and egg.

3 Heat oven to 350°F. In 13×9-inch (3-quart) glass baking dish, spoon $^2/_3$ cup of the Alfredo sauce. Place 4 noodles over sauce. Spread with half of cheese mixture and $2^1/_2$ cups of vegetable mixture; randomly spoon $^2/_3$ cup remaining sauce in dollops over noodles. Sprinkle with 1 cup of the mozzarella cheese. Top with 4 noodles. Spread with remaining cheese mixture and $2^1/_2$ cups vegetable mixture; randomly spoon $^2/_3$ cup sauce in dollops over vegetables. Sprinkle with 1 cup mozzarella cheese. Top with remaining 4 noodles and vegetable mixture; randomly spoon remaining sauce in dollops over top. Sprinkle with remaining 2 cups mozzarella cheese.

4 Bake uncovered 45 to 60 minutes or until bubbly and hot in center. Let stand 15 minutes before cutting.

If you want, use American cheese slices instead of the mozzarella.

1 Serving: Calories 730 (Calories from Fat 370); Total Fat 42g (Saturated Fat 24g); Cholesterol 150mg; Sodium 1050mg; Total Carbohydrate 52g (Dietary Fiber 5g); Protein 38g

Spinach Gnocchi with Nutmeg

Prep Time: 20 min ▪ Start to Finish: 1 hr 5 min ▪ 4 First-Course or 2 Main-Course Servings

Gnocchi

1 medium baking potato (6 oz)

1 teaspoon freshly grated nutmeg

1 egg

1 package (10 oz) frozen chopped spinach, thawed and squeezed to drain

1 to 1 1/3 cups all-purpose flour

Sauce and Topping

2 tablespoons butter or margarine

2 medium green onions, thinly sliced (2 tablespoons)

1 cup whipping cream

1/4 teaspoon white pepper

4 quarts water

1 tablespoon salt

1/4 cup freshly grated or shredded imported Parmesan cheese

1 Heat potato and water to cover to boiling. Cover and boil about 30 minutes or until tender; drain, cool slightly, peel and mash till smooth.

2 Add 1/2 teaspoon salt, nutmeg, egg, spinach and enough of the flour into mashed potato to make a stiff dough. Shape into 1-inch oval balls.

3 Melt butter in 10-inch skillet over medium-high heat. Add onions and cook 5 minutes or until tender. Stir in whipping cream and white pepper. Heat to boiling; reduce heat and simmer 10 minutes or until thickened.

4 Bring a 6-quart pot of salted water to boiling. Add gnocchi in two batches; cook each batch uncovered 4 minutes, remove with slotted spoon; and drain. Gently mix gnocchi with sauce and sprinkle with cheese.

1 Serving: Calories 435 (Calories from Fat 260); Total Fat 28g (Saturated Fat 17g); Cholesterol 140mg; Sodium 1710mg; Total Carbohydrate 35g (Dietary Fiber 3g); Protein 11g

Shrimp Creole

Prep Time: 30 min ▪ Start to Finish: 1 hr ▪ 6 Servings

2 lb uncooked medium shrimp in shells, thawed if frozen

1/4 cup butter or margarine

3 medium onions, chopped (1 1/2 cups)

2 medium green bell peppers, finely chopped (2 cups)

2 medium stalks celery, finely chopped (1 cup)

2 cloves garlic, finely chopped

1 cup water

2 teaspoons chopped fresh parsley

1 1/2 teaspoons salt

1/4 teaspoon ground red pepper (cayenne)

2 dried bay leaves

1 can (15 oz) tomato sauce

6 cups hot cooked rice

1 Peel shrimp. Make a shallow cut lengthwise down back of each shrimp; wash out vein. Cover and refrigerate.

2 In 3-quart saucepan, melt butter over medium heat. Cook onions, bell peppers, celery and garlic in butter about 10 minutes, stirring occasionally, until onions are tender.

3 Stir in remaining ingredients except rice and shrimp. Heat to boiling; reduce heat to low. Simmer uncovered 10 minutes.

4 Stir in shrimp. Heat to boiling; reduce heat to medium. Cover and cook 4 to 6 minutes, stirring occasionally, until shrimp are pink and firm. Remove bay leaves. Serve shrimp mixture over rice.

1 Serving: Calories 400 (Calories from Fat 80); Total Fat 9g (Saturated Fat 4.5g); Cholesterol 160mg; Sodium 1860mg; Total Carbohydrate 57g (Dietary Fiber 3g); Protein 22g

Cioppino (Italian Seafood Stew)

Prep Time: 20 min ▪ Start to Finish: 5 hrs 5 min ▪ 8 Servings

2 large onions, chopped (2 cups)
2 medium stalks celery, finely chopped (1 cup)
5 cloves garlic, finely chopped
1 can (28 oz) diced tomatoes, undrained
1 bottle (8 oz) clam juice
1 can (6 oz) tomato paste
$1/2$ cup dry white wine or water
1 tablespoon red wine vinegar
1 tablespoon olive or vegetable oil
$2^{1}/_{2}$ teaspoons Italian seasoning
$1/4$ teaspoon sugar
$1/4$ teaspoon crushed red pepper
1 dried bay leaf
1 pound firm-fleshed white fish, cut into 1-inch pieces
$3/4$ pound uncooked peeled deveined medium shrimp, thawed if frozen
1 can ($6^{1}/_{2}$ oz) chopped clams with juice, undrained
1 can (6 oz) crabmeat, drained, cartilage removed and flaked
$1/4$ cup chopped fresh parsley

1 Mix all ingredients except fish, shrimp, clams, crabmeat and parsley in 5- to 6-quart slow cooker.

2 Cover and cook on high heat setting 3 to 4 hours or until vegetables are tender.

3 Stir in fish, shrimp, clams and crabmeat. Cover and cook on low heat setting 30 to 45 minutes or until fish flakes easily with fork. Remove bay leaf. Stir in parsley.

1 Serving: Calories 200 (Calories from Fat 35); Total Fat 4g (Saturated Fat 1g); Cholesterol 125mg; Sodium 600mg; Total Carbohydrate 15g (Dietary Fiber 3g); Protein 29g

Bayou Gumbo

Prep Time: 25 min ▪ Start to Finish: 9 hrs 45 min ▪ 6 Servings

3 tablespoons vegetable oil

3 tablespoons all-purpose flour

1/2 pound smoked pork sausage, cut into 1/2-inch slices

2 cups frozen cut okra

1 large onion, chopped (1 cup)

1 large green bell pepper, chopped (1 1/2 cups)

3 cloves garlic, finely chopped

1/4 teaspoon ground red pepper (cayenne)

1/4 teaspoon pepper

1 can (14 1/2 oz) diced tomatoes, undrained

1 1/2 cups uncooked regular long-grain rice

3 cups water

1 package (12 oz) frozen cooked peeled and deveined medium shrimp,
    rinsed and drained

1 Heat oil in 1-quart saucepan over medium-high heat. Stir in flour. Cook 5 minutes, stirring constantly; reduce heat to medium. Cook about 10 minutes, stirring constantly, until mixture turns reddish brown.

2 Place flour-oil mixture in 3 1/2- to 4-quart slow cooker. Stir in remaining ingredients except shrimp, rice and water.

3 Cover and cook on low heat setting 7 to 9 hours.

4 Cook rice in water as directed on package. While rice is cooking, stir shrimp into gumbo mixture in slow cooker. Cover and cook on low heat setting 20 minutes. Serve gumbo over rice.

1 Serving: Calories 490 (Calories from Fat 180); Total Fat 20g (Saturated Fat 5g); Cholesterol 140mg; Sodium 720mg; Total Carbohydrate 54g (Dietary Fiber 4g); Protein 26g

Chicken Penne with Vodka Sauce

Prep Time: 20 min ▪ Start to Finish: 1 hr ▪ 6 Servings

3 tablespoons butter or margarine

1 tablespoon olive oil

2 cloves garlic, finely chopped

1 small onion, chopped ($^1/_4$ cup)

$^1/_4$ cup chopped prosciutto (about 2 oz)

2 boneless, skinless chicken breasts (about $^1/_2$ lb), cut into 1-inch pieces

$^1/_2$ cup vodka or chicken broth

$^1/_2$ cup whipping cream

$^1/_2$ cup sliced pitted imported kalamata or large pitted ripe olives

1 tablespoon chopped fresh parsley

$^1/_2$ teaspoon pepper

1 package (16 oz) uncooked penne pasta

$^1/_4$ cup freshly grated or shredded Parmesan cheese

1 Heat butter and oil in 10-inch skillet over medium-high heat. Cook garlic and onion in butter mixture about 5 minutes, stirring occasionally, until onion is tender.

2 Stir in prosciutto and chicken. Cook about 5 minutes, stirring occasionally, until chicken is brown. Stir in vodka. Cook uncovered until liquid has evaporated

3 Stir in whipping cream, olives, parsley and pepper. Heat to boiling; reduce heat. Simmer uncovered about 30 minutes, stirring frequently, until thickened.

4 While sauce is simmering, cook and drain pasta as directed on package. Add pasta to sauce; toss gently until pasta is evenly coated. Sprinkle with cheese.

Vodka in your pasta sauce? Trust us—it's a great way to use it!

1 Serving: Calories 530 (Calories from Fat 180); Total Fat 20g (Saturated Fat 9g); Cholesterol 70mg; Sodium 330mg; Total Carbohydrate 62g (Dietary Fiber 3g); Protein 23g

Chile-Chicken Tacos

Prep Time: 15 min ▪ Start to Finish: 7 hrs 30 min ▪ 12 Tacos

1 1/4 lb boneless, skinless chicken thighs
1 envelope (1.25 oz) taco seasoning mix
1 tablespoon packed brown sugar
1 can (4.5 oz) chopped green chiles
1 cup frozen corn (from 1-lb bag), thawed
1 can (10 oz) enchilada sauce
4 medium green onions, sliced (1/4 cup)
1 package (4.6 oz) taco shells, warmed if desired
3 cups shredded lettuce
1 medium tomato, chopped (3/4 cup)

1 Spray 3- to 4-quart slow cooker with cooking spray. Place chicken thighs in cooker. Sprinkle with taco seasoning mix and brown sugar; toss to coat. Mix in green chiles, corn and 1/2 cup of the enchilada sauce. Refrigerate remaining enchilada sauce.

2 Cover and cook on low heat setting 6 to 7 hours.

3 Place chicken on cutting board; use 2 forks to pull chicken into shreds. Return chicken to cooker. Stir in green onions. Cover and cook on low heat setting 15 minutes.

4 Heat remaining enchilada sauce. Serve chicken mixture in taco shells with lettuce, tomatoes and warm enchilada sauce.

1 Taco: Calories 170 (Calories from Fat 60); Total Fat 7g (Saturated Fat 1.5g); Cholesterol 30mg; Sodium 310mg; Total Carbohydrate 16g (Dietary Fiber 2g); Protein 12g

Picadillo Chicken Paella

Prep Time: 15 min ▪ Start to Finish: 1 hr 20 min ▪ 4 Servings

1 cup uncooked regular long-grain rice
$1/2$ lb smoked chorizo sausage, sliced
$1/4$ cup raisins
1 can ($14^{1}/_2$ oz) stewed tomatoes, undrained
1 can ($14^{1}/_2$ oz) chicken broth
$1/2$ teaspoon ground turmeric
4 chicken legs, skin removed if desired
4 chicken thighs, skin removed if desired
$1/4$ teaspoon seasoned salt
$1/4$ teaspoon paprika
1 cup frozen green peas, thawed

1 Heat oven to 375°F. Spray 13×9×2-inch baking dish with cooking spray.

2 Mix rice, sausage, raisins, tomatoes, broth and turmeric in baking dish. Arrange chicken on top; press into rice mixture. Sprinkle chicken with seasoned salt and paprika.

3 Cover and bake 30 minutes. Uncover and bake about 30 minutes longer or until liquid is absorbed and juice of chicken is no longer pink when centers of thickest pieces are cut. Stir in peas. Bake uncovered 5 minutes.

1 Serving: Calories 780 (Calories from Fat 340); Total Fat 38g (Saturated Fat 13g); Cholesterol 150mg; Sodium 1660mg; Total Carbohydrate 61g (Dietary Fiber 4g); Protein 53g

Southern Turkey and Lentil Casserole

Prep Time: 30 min ▪ Start to Finish: 1 hr 40 min ▪ 5 Servings

4 slices bacon, cut into ¹/₂-inch pieces
2 medium carrots, chopped (1 cup)
1 medium onion, chopped (¹/₂ cup)
1 cup dried lentils (8 oz), sorted and rinsed
1 can (15 to 16 oz) black-eyed peas, drained, rinsed
1 can (14¹/₂ oz) stewed tomatoes with garlic, oregano and basil, undrained
1 can (14¹/₂ oz) chicken broth
1¹/₂ cups ¹/₂-inch cubes cooked turkey or chicken
2 tablespoons chili sauce
Chopped fresh parsley, if desired

1 Heat oven to 350°F. Spray rectangular baking dish, 13×9×2 inches, with cooking spray.

2 Cook bacon, carrots and onion in 10-inch nonstick skillet over medium heat 3 to 5 minutes, stirring occasionally, until vegetables are crisp-tender. Stir in lentils. Cook 3 minutes, stirring occasionally.

3 Spoon mixture into baking dish. Stir in black-eyed peas, tomatoes, broth, turkey and chili sauce.

4 Cover and bake 60 to 70 minutes or until liquid is absorbed. Sprinkle with parsley.

1 Serving: Calories 330 (Calories from Fat 65); Total Fat 7g (Saturated Fat 2g); Cholesterol 40mg; Sodium 990mg; Total Carbohydrate 51g (Dietary Fiber 16g); Protein 32g

You can use ketchup in place of the chili sauce in this delicious casserole.

Jamaican Jerk Pork Chops with Mango Salsa

Prep Time: 30 min ▪ Start to Finish: 1 hr ▪ 4 Servings

Jamaican Jerk Seasoning

2 teaspoons dried thyme leaves

1 teaspoon ground allspice

1 teaspoon brown sugar

$1/2$ teaspoon salt

$1/2$ teaspoon cracked black pepper

$1/4$ to $1/2$ teaspoon ground red pepper (cayenne)

$1/4$ teaspoon crushed dried sage leaves

4 cloves garlic, finely chopped

Pork Chops

4 pork loin or rib chops, about $3/4$ inch thick (about 2 lb)

Mango Salsa

1 medium mango, cut lengthwise in half, seed removed and chopped (1 cup)

$1/4$ cup finely chopped red onion

1 tablespoon finely chopped fresh or 1 teaspoon dried mint leaves

1 small jalapeño chile, finely chopped (2 to 3 teaspoons)

2 tablespoons lime juice

$1/8$ teaspoon salt

1 Make Jamaican Jerk Seasoning by mixing all ingredients in small bowl. Rub seasoning into pork chops. Cover and refrigerate at least 30 minutes but no longer than 1 hour.

2 Meanwhile, make Mango Salsa by mixing all ingredients in small glass or plastic bowl. Cover and refrigerate until serving.

3 Heat coals or gas grill for direct heat.

4 Cover and grill pork chops over medium heat 9 to 12 minutes, turning once, until no longer pink when cut near bone. Serve with salsa.

1 serving: Calories 215 (Calories from Fat 70); Total Fat 8g (Saturated Fat 3g); Cholesterol 65mg; Sodium 410mg; Total Carbohydrate 14g (Dietary Fiber 2g); Protein 24g

Instead of making your own jerk seasoning, use 2 tablespoons of purchased Jamaican Jerk Blend seasoning. You'll find it in the spice aisle of your supermarket.

Slow-Cooked Pork Burrito Bowls

Prep Time: 15 min ■ Start to Finish: 8 hrs 15 min ■ 10 Servings

2-lb boneless pork shoulder roast
1 can (15 to 16 oz) pinto beans, drained, rinsed
2 tablespoons taco seasoning mix (from 1.25-oz package)
1 can (4.5 oz) diced green chiles, undrained
2 packages (7.6 oz each) Spanish rice mix
5 cups water
1 tablespoon butter or margarine
1½ cups shredded Mexican blend cheese (6 oz)
2¼ cups shredded lettuce
½ cup chunky salsa

1 If pork roast comes in netting or is tied, remove netting or strings. In 3- to 4-quart slow cooker, place pork. Pour beans around pork. Sprinkle taco seasoning mix over pork. Pour green chiles over beans.

2 Cover and cook on low heat setting 8 to 10 hours.

3 About 45 minutes before serving, in 3-quart saucepan, make rice mixes as directed on package, using water and butter.

4 Remove pork from cooker; place on cutting board. Use 2 forks to pull pork into shreds. Return pork to cooker; gently stir to mix with beans.

5 To serve, spoon rice into each serving bowl and top with pork mixture, cheese, lettuce and salsa.

1 Serving: Calories 450 (Calories from Fat 160); Total Fat 18g (Saturated Fat 8g); Cholesterol 75mg; Sodium 1050mg; Total Carbohydrate 46g (Dietary Fiber 5g); Protein 30g

Provençal Pork Roast

Prep Time: 15 min ▪ Start to Finish: 9 hrs 30 min ▪ 8 Servings

3- to 3^1/$_2$-lb pork boneless loin roast
1 teaspoon seasoned salt
^{1}/$_2$ teaspoon garlic-pepper blend
6 to 8 small red potatoes, quartered
1 can (14.5 oz) diced tomatoes with Italian seasonings, undrained
2 tablespoons all-purpose flour
1 medium zucchini, cut lengthwise in half, then cut crosswise into slices (2 cups)
^{1}/$_2$ cup halved pitted ripe olives, if desired

1 Spray 12-inch nonstick skillet with cooking spray. If pork roast comes in netting or is tied, do not remove. Sprinkle pork with seasoned salt and garlic-pepper blend. Cook pork in skillet over medium-high heat 5 to 6 minutes, turning occasionally, until brown on all sides.

2 Spray 5- to 6-quart slow cooker with cooking spray. Place pork in cooker. Arrange potatoes around pork. Mix tomatoes and flour in small bowl; pour over pork and potatoes. Cover and cook on low heat setting 8 to 9 hours.

3 Place pork and potatoes on platter; cover to keep warm. Add zucchini and olives to sauce in cooker. Increase heat setting to high. Cover and cook 10 to 15 minutes or until zucchini is tender. Remove netting or strings from pork. Serve pork with zucchini mixture.

Don't have Italian-seasoned tomatoes on hand? Use a can of plain diced tomatoes and stir in ^{1}/$_2$ teaspoon Italian seasoning.

1 Serving: Calories 360 (Calories from Fat 120); Total Fat 13g (Saturated Fat 4.5g); Cholesterol 110mg; Sodium 380mg; Total Carbohydrate 20g (Dietary Fiber 3g); Protein 40g

Barbecued Ribs

Prep Time: 15 min ▪ Start to Finish: 10 hrs 15 min ▪ 4 Servings

3¹/₂ lb pork loin back ribs
¹/₄ cup packed brown sugar
¹/₂ teaspoon pepper
3 tablespoons liquid smoke
2 cloves garlic, chopped
1 teaspoon salt
1 medium onion, sliced
¹/₂ cup carbonated beverage
1¹/₂ cups barbecue sauce

1 Spray inside of 4- to 5-quart slow cooker with cooking spray.

2 Remove inner skin from ribs. Mix brown sugar, pepper, liquid smoke, garlic and salt; rub mixture into ribs. Cut ribs into 4-inch pieces. Layer ribs and onion in slow cooker. Pour cola over ribs.

3 Cover and cook on low heat setting 8 to 9 hours or until tender. Remove ribs from slow cooker. Drain and discard liquid.

4 Pour barbecue sauce into shallow bowl. Dip ribs into sauce. Place ribs in slow cooker. Pour any remaining sauce over ribs. Cover and cook on low heat setting 1 hour.

Spraying the inside of the slow cooker with cooking spray
makes cleanup a snap.

1 Serving: Calories 890 (Calories from Fat 540); Total Fat 60g (Saturated Fat 22g); Cholesterol 230mg; Sodium 1540mg; Total Carbohydrate 32g (Dietary Fiber 2g); Protein 58g

Beef Tagine

Prep Time: 30 min ▪ Start to Finish: 1 hr 50 min ▪ 4 Servings

1 boneless beef chuck roast (2 lb), cut into 1-inch cubes	1 cup pitted prunes
1½ teaspoons salt	¼ cup honey
1 tablespoon vegetable oil	¾ teaspoon ground cinnamon
1 medium onion, chopped (½ cup)	½ teaspoon ground cumin
2 cloves garlic, finely chopped	¼ cup slivered almonds
3½ cups chicken broth	Juice of 1 lemon (3 tablespoons)
1 teaspoon ground ginger	½ teaspoon orange flower water, if desired
1 teaspoon freshly ground pepper	2 tablespoons chopped fresh parsley
½ teaspoon saffron threads, if desired, crushed	Hot cooked couscous or brown rice, if desired

1 Sprinkle beef with ½ teaspoon of the salt.

2 In 4- or 5-quart Dutch oven, heat oil over medium-high heat until hot. Add half of the beef and cook 4 minutes, stirring occasionally, until evenly browned. Use slotted spoon to remove beef and place in bowl. Repeat with remaining beef.

3 Add additional oil to pan if necessary. Add onion and cook 4 minutes, stirring constantly, until soft. Add garlic and cook 30 seconds, stirring constantly.

4 Return beef to pan. Stir in broth, ginger, pepper, remaining 1 teaspoon salt and the saffron. Heat to boiling, stirring occasionally. Reduce heat to low. Gently simmer uncovered 1 hour, stirring occasionally.

5 Stir in prunes, honey, cinnamon and cumin. Cook uncovered 20 to 25 minutes, stirring occasionally, until beef is tender and prunes are plumped but not falling apart.

6 Stir in almonds, lemon juice and orange flower water. Sprinkle with parsley and serve over couscous.

1 Serving: Calories 560 (Calories from Fat 220); Total Fat 24g (Saturated Fat 7g); Cholesterol 85mg; Sodium 1850mg; Total Carbohydrate 51g (Dietary Fiber 5g); Protein 35g

Curried Coconut Beef with Winter Vegetables

Prep Time: 25 min ■ Start to Finish: 1 hr 55 min ■ 6 Servings

1 tablespoon vegetable oil

2 lb beef stew meat

1 large onion, chopped (1 cup)

2 cloves garlic, finely chopped

1½ tablespoons curry powder

1 can (14 oz) coconut milk (not cream of coconut)

1 tablespoon packed brown sugar

2 tablespoons lemon juice

3 medium carrots, chopped (1½ cups)

2 medium parsnips, peeled and chopped (1 cup)

1½ cups chopped peeled sweet potatoes

1 teaspoon salt

¼ teaspoon pepper

Chopped fresh cilantro, if desired

1 Heat oven to 350°F. Heat oil in 4-quart ovenproof Dutch oven over medium-high heat. Cook beef in oil, stirring occasionally, until brown.

2 Stir in onion and garlic. Cook 2 to 3 minutes, stirring occasionally, until onion is crisp-tender. Stir in curry powder, coconut milk, brown sugar and lemon juice. Cover and place in oven; bake about 1 hour or until beef is tender.

3 Stir in remaining ingredients except cilantro. Cover and bake about 30 minutes or until vegetables are tender. Garnish with cilantro.

This is perfect for a cozy winter supper. Add a crisp green salad, warm dinner rolls and hot coffee, cider or tea to round out the meal.

1 Serving: Calories 495 (Calories from Fat 260); Total Fat 29g (Saturated Fat 16g); Cholesterol 80mg; Sodium 510mg; Total Carbohydrate 35g (Dietary Fiber 7g); Protein 30g

5

say cheese!

Southwest Cheese Soup

Prep Time: 20 min ▪ Start to Finish: 20 min ▪ 4 Servings

1 loaf (1 lb) prepared cheese product, cut into cubes
1 can (15.25 oz) whole kernel corn, drained
1 can (15 oz) black beans, drained, rinsed
1 can (10 oz) diced tomatoes with green chiles, undrained
1 cup milk
Fresh cilantro sprigs, if desired

1 In 4-quart saucepan, mix all ingredients except cilantro.

2 Cook over medium-low heat 10 to 15 minutes, stirring frequently, until cheese is melted and soup is hot. Garnish each serving with cilantro.

Enjoy this unbelievably easy cheese soup with warm cornbread.

1 Serving: Calories 610 (Calories from Fat 250); Total Fat 28g (Saturated Fat 17g); Cholesterol 95mg; Sodium 2130mg; Total Carbohydrate 59g (Dietary Fiber 9g); Protein 32g

Southwest Chicken Nachos

Prep Time: 15 min ▪ Start to Finish: 4 hrs 45 min ▪ 21 Servings

1 package (16 oz) mild Mexican pasteurized prepared cheese product with jalapeño
    peppers, cut into cubes
³/₄ cup salsa
1 can (15 oz) black beans, rinsed and drained
1 package (8 oz) frozen cooked Southwest-seasoned chicken breast strips, thawed
    and cubed
1 container (8 oz) Southwest ranch sour cream dip
1 medium green bell pepper, chopped (1 cup)
1 medium red bell pepper, chopped (1 cup)
12 oz large tortilla chips

1 Place cheese, salsa, beans and chicken in 3- to 4-quart slow cooker.

2 Cover and cook on low heat setting 3 to 4 hours, stirring halfway through cooking, until cheese is melted and mixture is hot.

3 Stir in sour cream dip and bell peppers. Increase heat setting to high. Cover and cook about 30 minutes or until mixture is hot. Serve over tortilla chips. Topping will hold on low heat setting up to 2 hours; stir occasionally.

Cut the cheese into chunks that are about the same size so
    they'll melt evenly.

1 Serving: Calories 230 (Calories from Fat 110); Total Fat 12g (Saturated Fat 5g); Cholesterol 30mg;
Sodium 600mg; Total Carbohydrate 20g (Dietary Fiber 2g); Protein 11g

Veggie Quesadillas

Prep Time: 15 min ■ Start to Finish: 20 min ■ 4 Servings (1 quesadilla each)

1 cup shredded zucchini
1 small tomato, seeded, chopped ($^1/_2$ cup)
1 tablespoon chopped fresh or 1 teaspoon dried oregano leaves
$^1/_2$ teaspoon garlic-pepper blend
8 whole wheat flour tortillas (8 inch)
2 cups shredded Italian cheese blend (8 oz)
Tomato pasta sauce or marinara sauce, heated, if desired

1 Heat oven to 350°F. In medium bowl, mix zucchini, tomato, oregano and garlic-pepper blend.

2 On ungreased large cookie sheet, place 4 tortillas. Sprinkle $^1/_2$ cup of the cheese evenly over each of the 4 tortillas. Spoon $^1/_4$ of the vegetable mixture over cheese. Top with remaining tortillas.

3 Bake about 6 minutes or until hot and cheese is melted. Cut each quesadilla into 6 to 8 wedges. Serve with pasta sauce.

1 Serving: Calories 300 (Calories from Fat 150); Total Fat 16g (Saturated Fat 10g); Cholesterol 40mg; Sodium 680mg; Total Carbohydrate 20g (Dietary Fiber 4g); Protein 18g

Cheese Enchiladas

Prep Time: 25 min ▪ Start to Finish: 45 min ▪ 4 Servings

2 cups shredded Monterey Jack
    cheese (8 oz)
1 cup shredded Cheddar cheese (4 oz)
1/2 cup sour cream
1 medium onion, chopped (1/2 cup)
2 tablespoons chopped fresh parsley
1/4 teaspoon pepper
1 can (15 oz) tomato sauce
1 small green bell pepper, chopped
    (1/2 cup)
1 can (4.5 oz) chopped green chiles,
    drained

1 clove garlic, finely chopped
2/3 cup water
1 tablespoon chili powder
1 1/2 teaspoons chopped fresh or
    1/2 teaspoon dried oregano
    leaves
1/4 teaspoon ground cumin
8 corn tortillas (5 or 6 inch)
Additional shredded cheese,
    sour cream and chopped
    onion, if desired

1 Heat oven to 350°F. In medium bowl, mix cheeses, sour cream, onion, parsley and pepper; set aside.

2 In 2-quart saucepan, heat tomato sauce, bell pepper, chiles, garlic, water, chili powder, oregano and cumin to boiling, stirring occasionally; reduce heat. Simmer uncovered 5 minutes. Pour into ungreased 9-inch glass pie plate.

3 Dip each tortilla into sauce to coat both sides. Spoon about 1/4 cup cheese mixture onto each tortilla; roll tortilla around filling. Place seam side down in ungreased 11×7-inch glass baking dish. Pour remaining sauce over enchiladas.

4 Bake uncovered about 20 minutes or until bubbly. Garnish with additional shredded cheese, sour cream and chopped onion.

1 Serving: Calories 530 (Calories from Fat 300); Total Fat 34g (Saturated Fat 20g); Cholesterol 100mg; Sodium 1310mg; Total Carbohydrate 31g (Dietary Fiber 5g); Protein 26g

Toasted Cheese, Avocado and Tomato Sandwiches

Prep Time: 15 min ▪ Start to Finish: 15 min ▪ 4 Sandwiches

8 slices pumpernickel bread
2 to 3 tablespoons creamy Dijon mustard-mayonnaise spread
1 medium avocado, pitted, peeled and thinly sliced
1 medium tomato, thinly sliced
4 slices (1 oz each) Colby–Monterey Jack cheese blend
2 tablespoons butter or margarine

1 Spread each slice of bread with mustard-mayonnaise spread. Top 4 slices with avocado, tomato and cheese. Top with remaining bread slices, spread side down.

2 In 12-inch skillet, melt butter over medium heat. Add sandwiches; cover and cook 4 to 5 minutes, turning once, until both sides are crisp and cheese is melted.

1 Sandwich: Calories 380 (Calories from Fat 210); Total Fat 23g (Saturated Fat 10g); Cholesterol 40mg; Sodium 660mg; Total Carbohydrate 32g (Dietary Fiber 5g); Protein 13g

Onion and Bacon Grilled Cheese Sandwiches

Prep Time: 25 min ▪ Start to Finish: 25 min ▪ 4 Sandwiches

4 slices bacon, cut into ½-inch pieces
1 medium onion, thinly sliced
8 slices (1 oz each) Cheddar cheese
8 slices Vienna bread, ½ inch thick

1 In 12-inch nonstick skillet, cook bacon over medium heat about 4 minutes, stirring occasionally, until almost cooked.

2 Add onion to skillet. Cook 2 to 3 minutes, turning occasionally, until tender. Remove bacon and onion from skillet. Reserve 1 tablespoon drippings in skillet.

3 To make each sandwich, layer cheese, bacon and onion between 2 bread slices. Place 2 sandwiches in drippings in skillet. Cover; cook over medium-low heat 3 to 5 minutes, turning once, until bread is crisp and golden brown and cheese is melted. Repeat with remaining sandwiches.

The Vienna bread is great here, but feel free to use whatever bread you like best.

1 Sandwich: Calories 350 (Calories from Fat 170); Total Fat 19g (Saturated Fat 10g); Cholesterol 55mg; Sodium 730mg; Total Carbohydrate 27g (Dietary Fiber 2g); Protein 18g

Cheese Steak Sandwiches with Sautéed Onions and Peppers

Prep Time: 10 min ▪ Start to Finish: 25 min ▪ 6 Sandwiches

3 tablespoons olive oil

2 tablespoons butter

2 medium onions, thinly sliced

2 red bell peppers, thinly sliced

2 lb beef top round (about 1¹/₂ inch thick), cut lengthwise into paper-thin strips

¹/₂ teaspoon salt

¹/₂ teaspoon pepper

2 teaspoons Worcestershire sauce

6 hoagie buns, split

1¹/₄ cups cheese dip (from 15-oz jar)

1 In 10-inch skillet, heat 1¹/₂ tablespoons of the oil and 1 tablespoon of the butter over medium heat until hot. Add onions and bell peppers. Cook about 10 minutes, stirring occasionally, until golden brown and tender. Remove and set aside.

2 Toss beef with salt and pepper. To the same skillet, add remaining oil and butter and increase heat to medium-high. Add one-fourth of the beef and cook 1 to 2 minutes, turning once, until beef is browned. Remove beef from skillet, and repeat to cook remaining beef.

3 Return beef to skillet with onions and bell peppers. Stir in Worcestershire sauce. Divide beef evenly among bottom halves of buns and spoon 3 tablespoons cheese dip onto each. Cover with top halves of buns. (If your cheese dip has been refrigerated, spoon it into a microwavable bowl and microwave 10 to 20 seconds on High or until warm).

1 Sandwich: Calories 530 (Calories from Fat 220); Total Fat 24g (Saturated Fat 8g); Cholesterol 100mg; Sodium 930mg; Total Carbohydrate 41g (Dietary Fiber 3g); Protein 38g

Grilled Cheddar-Stuffed Chicken Breasts

Prep Time: 30 min ▪ Start to Finish: 30 min ▪ 4 Servings

4 boneless skinless chicken breasts (about 1¼ lb)
¼ teaspoon salt
¼ teaspoon pepper
1 piece (3 oz) Cheddar cheese
1 tablespoon butter or margarine, melted
¼ cup chunky-style salsa

1 Heat gas or charcoal grill. Between pieces of plastic wrap or waxed paper, place each chicken breast smooth side down; gently pound with flat side of meat mallet or rolling pin until about ¼ inch thick. Sprinkle with salt and pepper.

2 Cut cheese into 4 slices, about 3×1×¼ inch. Place 1 slice cheese on center of each chicken piece. Roll chicken around cheese, folding in sides. Brush rolls with butter.

3 Place chicken rolls, seam sides down, on grill. Cover grill; cook over medium heat about 15 minutes, turning after 10 minutes, until chicken is no longer pink in center. Serve with salsa.

Add a peppery punch to this easy chicken dish by using Monterey Jack cheese with jalapeño chiles instead of the Cheddar cheese.

1 Serving: Calories 280 (Calories from Fat 130); Total Fat 15g (Saturated Fat 8g); Cholesterol 115mg; Sodium 450mg; Total Carbohydrate 1g (Dietary Fiber 0g); Protein 37g

Cheesy Chicken and Rotini Casserole

Prep Time: 15 min ■ Start to Finish: 1 hr ■ 6 Servings

3 cups uncooked rotini pasta (9 oz)

2 cups cut-up cooked chicken

1 cup frozen onions, celery, bell pepper and parsley (from 16-oz bag)

1 can (10¾ oz) condensed cream of chicken soup

1 cup chicken broth

2 plum (Roma) tomatoes, each cut into 6 wedges

3 medium green onions, sliced (3 tablespoons)

½ cup shredded Cheddar cheese (2 oz)

1 Heat oven to 350°F. Grease square pan, 8×8×2 inches. Cook and drain pasta as directed on package.

2 Mix pasta, chicken, frozen vegetables, soup and broth in pan. Bake uncovered 35 to 40 minutes or until bubbly around edges.

3 Top with tomatoes. Sprinkle with onions and cheese. Bake uncovered about 3 minutes or until cheese is melted.

1 Serving: Calories 365 (Calories from Fat 100); Total Fat 11g (Saturated Fat 4g); Cholesterol 50mg; Sodium 760mg; Total Carbohydrate 44g (Dietary Fiber 2g); Protein 25g

Mushroom fans—go ahead and make this casserole with cream of mushroom soup.

Four-Cheese Mashed Potato Casserole

Prep Time: 25 min ▪ Start to Finish: 1 hr 35 min ▪ 24 Servings (½ cup each)

5 lb white potatoes, peeled, cut into 1-inch pieces (about 14 cups)
3 oz (from 8-oz package) reduced-fat cream cheese (Neufchâtel), softened
¼ cup crumbled blue cheese
1 cup shredded reduced-fat Cheddar cheese (4 oz)
¼ cup shredded Parmesan cheese
1 container (8 oz) reduced-fat sour cream
1 teaspoon garlic salt
¼ teaspoon paprika
1 teaspoon chopped fresh chives, if desired

1 In 6-quart saucepan or Dutch oven, place potatoes. Add enough water to cover potatoes. Heat to boiling over high heat; reduce heat to medium. Cook uncovered 15 to 18 minutes or until tender; drain. Mash potatoes in saucepan with potato masher or electric mixer on low speed.

2 Meanwhile, in large bowl, beat cream cheese, blue cheese, Cheddar cheese and Parmesan cheese with electric mixer on low speed until smooth. Beat in sour cream and garlic salt.

3 Heat oven to 350°F. Stir cheese mixture into mashed potatoes until well blended. If potatoes are too stiff, stir in milk, 1 tablespoon at a time, until desired consistency. Spoon into ungreased 13×9-inch (3-quart) glass baking dish.

4 Bake uncovered 35 to 40 minutes or until hot and top is lightly browned. Sprinkle with paprika and chives.

1 Serving: Calories 110 (Calories from Fat 25); Total Fat 3g (Saturated Fat 2g); Cholesterol 10mg; Sodium 140mg; Total Carbohydrate 18g (Dietary Fiber 2g); Protein 4g

Cheese and
potatoes—
a marriage made
in heaven!

Cheesy Pizza Casserole

Prep Time: 15 min ■ Start to Finish: 50 min ■ 6 Servings

3 cups uncooked rigatoni pasta (9 oz)
1/2 pound ground beef
1/4 cup sliced ripe olives
1 can (4 oz) mushroom pieces and stems, drained
1 jar (26 to 28 oz) vegetable primavera pasta sauce
1 cup shredded mozzarella cheese (4 oz)

1 Heat oven to 350°F. Cook and drain pasta as directed on package.

2 While pasta is cooking, cook beef in 10-inch skillet over medium-high heat, stirring occasionally, until brown; drain. Mix pasta, beef and remaining ingredients except cheese in ungreased 2 1/2-quart casserole.

3 Cover and bake about 30 minutes or until hot and bubbly. Sprinkle with cheese. Bake uncovered about 5 minutes or until cheese is melted.

1 Serving: Calories 490 (Calories from Fat 135); Total Fat 15g (Saturated Fat 5g); Cholesterol 30mg; Sodium 970mg; Total Carbohydrate 72g (Dietary Fiber 5g); Protein 22g

Italian Sausage Calzone

Prep Time: 30 min ▪ Start to Finish: 55 min ▪ 4 Servings

$^1/_2$ pound bulk Italian sausage

1 small onion, chopped ($^1/_4$ cup)

$^1/_3$ cup pizza sauce

1 can (2 oz) mushroom pieces and stems, drained (about $^1/_4$ cup)

2 cups Original Bisquick baking mix

$^1/_3$ cup hot water

1 tablespoon vegetable oil

1 cup shredded mozzarella cheese (4 oz)

$^1/_4$ cup grated Parmesan cheese

1 large egg white

1 Heat oven to 450°F. Cook sausage in 10-inch skillet over medium heat, stirring occasionally, until no longer pink; drain. Stir in onion, pizza sauce and mushrooms; remove from heat.

2 Mix baking mix, water and oil until dough forms. Roll dough into 12-inch circle on cloth-covered surface dusted with baking mix. Place dough on ungreased cookie sheet.

3 Top half of the dough circle with mozzarella cheese, sausage mixture and Parmesan cheese to within 1 inch of edge. Fold dough over filling; pinch edges or press with fork to seal securely. Brush with egg white.

4 Bake 15 to 20 minutes or until golden brown. Cool 5 minutes. Cut into wedges.

Calzones are stuffed sandwiches—they make great finger food, full of gooey cheese and hearty sausage.

1 Serving: Calories 570 (Calories from Fat 305); Total Fat 34g (Saturated Fat 12g); Cholesterol 65mg; Sodium 1760mg; Total Carbohydrate 41g (Dietary Fiber 1g); Protein 26g

Cheesy Italian Tortellini

Prep Time: 15 min ▪ Start to Finish: 8 hrs 30 min ▪ 4 to 6 Servings

$^1/_2$ lb ground beef
$^1/_2$ lb bulk Italian sausage
1 container (15 oz) refrigerated marinara sauce
1 cup sliced fresh mushrooms
1 can (14$^1/_2$ oz) diced tomatoes with Italian herbs, undrained
1 package (9 oz) refrigerated cheese-filled tortellini
1 cup shredded mozzarella cheese or pizza cheese blend (4 oz)

1 Cook beef and sausage in 10-inch skillet over medium heat about 10 minutes, stirring occasionally, until brown; drain.

2 Spray inside of 4- to 5-quart slow cooker with cooking spray. Mix beef mixture, marinara sauce, mushrooms and tomatoes in slow cooker.

3 Cover and cook on low heat setting 7 to 8 hours.

4 Stir in tortellini; sprinkle with cheese. Cover and cook on low heat setting about 15 minutes longer or until tortellini is tender.

Try different flavors of marinara sauce, such as roasted garlic or peppers and onion, for an added burst of flavor.

1 Serving: Calories 575 (Calories from Fat 295); Total Fat 33g (Saturated Fat 13g); Cholesterol 135mg; Sodium 1330mg; Total Carbohydrate 39g (Dietary Fiber 3g); Protein 34g

Four-Cheese Risotto

Prep Time: 55 min ▪ Start to Finish: 55 min ▪ 4 Servings

7 cups vegetable broth
1/4 cup olive or vegetable oil
1 large onion, chopped (1 cup)
2 cups uncooked Arborio or medium-grain white rice
2 tablespoons dry white wine or vegetable broth
1 cup ricotta cheese
1/2 cup shredded mozzarella cheese (2 oz)
1/2 cup crumbled Gorgonzola or blue cheese
1/2 cup grated or shredded Parmesan cheese
2 tablespoons chopped fresh parsley

1 In 3-quart saucepan, heat broth over medium heat.

2 Meanwhile, in 12-inch nonstick skillet or 4-quart saucepan, heat oil over medium-high heat. Add onion; cook about 5 minutes, stirring frequently, until tender.

3 Stir in rice. Cook about 5 minutes, stirring occasionally, until edges of kernels are translucent. Stir in wine. Cook about 3 minutes, stirring constantly, until wine is absorbed.

4 Reduce heat to medium. Pour 1/2 cup of the hot broth over rice mixture. Cook uncovered, stirring frequently, until broth is absorbed. Continue cooking 30 to 35 minutes, adding broth 1/2 cup at a time and stirring frequently, until rice is almost tender and mixture is creamy. Remove from heat.

5 Stir in cheeses. Sprinkle with parsley.

1 Serving: Calories 760 (Calories from Fat 280); Total Fat 31g (Saturated Fat 12g); Cholesterol 50mg; Sodium 2370mg; Total Carbohydrate 93g (Dietary Fiber 2g); Protein 28g

Manicotti

Prep Time: 40 min ▪ Start to Finish: 1 hr 35 min ▪ 7 Servings

14 uncooked manicotti shells
1 lb lean (at least 80%) ground beef
1 large onion, chopped (1 cup)
2 cloves garlic, finely chopped
1 jar (26 to 30 oz) tomato pasta sauce
(any variety)
2 boxes (10 oz each) frozen chopped spinach,
thawed
2 cups small curd cottage cheese

2 cans (4 oz each) mushroom
pieces and stems, drained
1/3 cup grated Parmesan cheese
1/4 teaspoon ground nutmeg
1/4 teaspoon pepper
2 cups shredded mozzarella
cheese (8 oz)
2 tablespoons grated
Parmesan cheese

1 Cook and drain manicotti as directed on package using minimum cooking time (cooking for the minimum time helps prevent the shells from tearing while filling).

2 Meanwhile, in 10-inch skillet, cook beef, onion and garlic over medium heat 8 to 10 minutes, stirring occasionally, until beef is brown; drain. Stir in pasta sauce.

3 Heat oven to 350°F. Spray 13×9-inch glass baking dish with cooking spray.

4 Squeeze thawed spinach to drain; spread on paper towels and pat dry. In medium bowl, mix spinach, cottage cheese, mushrooms, 1/3 cup Parmesan cheese, the nutmeg and pepper.

5 In baking dish, spread 1 cup of the beef mixture. Fill manicotti shells with spinach mixture. Place shells on beef mixture in dish. Pour remaining beef mixture evenly over shells, covering shells completely. Sprinkle with mozzarella cheese and 2 tablespoons Parmesan cheese.

6 Cover and bake 30 minutes. Uncover and bake 20 to 25 minutes longer or until hot and bubbly.

1 Serving: Calories 570 (Calories from Fat 190); Total Fat 21g (Saturated Fat 10g); Cholesterol 70mg; Sodium 1360mg; Total Carbohydrate 55g (Dietary Fiber 6g); Protein 39g

Cheesy Vegetable Shells

Prep Time: 20 min ▪ Start to Finish: 1 hr ▪ 5 Servings (3 shells each)

15 uncooked jumbo pasta shells
1 can (15 oz) chunky tomato sauce
1 can (8 oz) tomato sauce
1 teaspoon olive or vegetable oil
$1/2$ cup shredded carrot (1 small)
$1/2$ cup shredded yellow summer squash (1 small)
$1/2$ cup sliced mushrooms (2 oz)
$1/4$ cup sliced green onions (3 medium)
1 clove garlic, finely chopped
2 cups nonfat or low-fat ricotta cheese (about 15 oz)
$1/4$ cup grated Parmesan cheese
$1/4$ cup cholesterol-free egg product or 2 egg whites, slightly beaten
2 tablespoons chopped fresh or 2 teaspoons dried basil leaves
$1/2$ cup shredded reduced-fat mozzarella cheese (2 oz)

1 Heat oven to 350°F. Spray rectangular baking dish, 11×7×1$1/2$ inches, with nonstick cooking spray. Cook and drain pasta shells as directed on package. Spoon half of the tomatoes into baking dish.

2 Heat oil in 10-inch nonstick skillet over medium-high heat. Cook carrot, squash, mushrooms, onions and garlic in oil, stirring frequently, until vegetables are crisp-tender. Stir in remaining ingredients except mozzarella cheese.

3 Fill shells with vegetable mixture. Place in baking dish. Spoon remaining tomatoes over shells. Sprinkle with mozzarella cheese. Cover and bake 40 to 45 minutes or until hot and bubbly. Sprinkle with shredded Parmesan cheese if desired.

1 Serving: Calories 260 (Calories from Fat 45); Total Fat 5g (Saturated Fat 3g); Cholesterol 5mg; Sodium 540mg; Total Carbohydrate 33g (Dietary Fiber 2g); Protein 23g

Southwest Cheese 'n' Pasta

Prep Time: 20 min ▪ Start to Finish: 20 min ▪ 6 Servings

2²/₃ cups uncooked cavatappi pasta (about 8 oz)
1 cup green salsa (salsa verde)
1¹/₂ cups milk
1 can (14.75 oz) cream-style corn, undrained
1 can (11 oz) whole kernel corn with red and green peppers, drained
1 loaf (8 oz) prepared cheese product, cut into cubes

1 In 12-inch nonstick skillet, mix all ingredients except cheese. Heat to boiling, stirring occasionally; reduce heat to low. Cover; cook 10 to 14 minutes, stirring frequently, until pasta is tender.

2 Stir in cheese until melted.

Ham it up for a heartier rendition of this cheesy dish! Add 2 cups of cubed cooked ham in Step 1, and continue as directed.

1 Serving: Calories 420 (Calories from Fat 100); Total Fat 12g (Saturated Fat 6g); Cholesterol 35mg; Sodium 950mg; Total Carbohydrate 61g (Dietary Fiber 5g); Protein 17g

Mexican Macaroni and Cheese

Prep Time: 20 min ▪ Start to Finish: 20 min ▪ 4 Servings

2 cups uncooked small macaroni shells (about 7 oz)
½ cup shredded reduced-fat Cheddar cheese (2 oz)
¼ cup sliced ripe olives
½ cup fat-free (skim) milk
½ teaspoon salt
1 small red bell pepper, chopped (½ cup)
1 can (4 oz) chopped green chiles, drained

1 Cook and drain macaroni as directed on package. Stir in remaining ingredients. Cook over low heat about 5 minutes, stirring occasionally, until cheese is melted and sauce is hot.

Can you say "olé"? This is a fun version of the classic mac 'n' cheese.

1 Serving: Calories 250 (Calories from Fat 35); Total Fat 4g (Saturated Fat 2g); Cholesterol 10mg; Sodium 720mg; Total Carbohydrate 43g (Dietary Fiber 2g); Protein 12g

Cheesy Vegetable Crepes

Prep Time: 35 min ▪ Start to Finish: 50 min ▪ 6 Servings (2 crepes each)

Vegetable Filling

2 tablespoons vegetable oil
2 medium zucchini, coarsely chopped (3 to 4 cups)
1/2 cup chopped green bell pepper
4 medium green onions, sliced (1/4 cup)
1/4 teaspoon instant minced garlic
2 medium tomatoes, coarsely chopped (1 1/2 cups)
1/2 teaspoon salt

Crepes

1 cup Original Bisquick
    baking mix
3/4 cup milk
2 eggs
1 cup grated Parmesan
    cheese

1 In 10-inch skillet, heat oil over medium heat. Cover and cook zucchini, bell pepper, onions and garlic in oil 3 to 5 minutes, stirring occasionally, until vegetables are crisp-tender; remove from heat. Stir in tomatoes. Sprinkle with salt. Cover and let stand 2 to 3 minutes.

2 Lightly grease 6- or 7-inch skillet; heat over medium-high heat. Stir Bisquick mix, milk and eggs in medium bowl with wire whisk or fork until blended.

3 Heat oven to 350°F. For each crepe, pour 2 tablespoons batter into hot skillet; rotate skillet until batter covers bottom. Cook until golden brown. Gently loosen edge with metal spatula; turn and cook other side until golden brown. Stack crepes, placing waxed paper between, as you remove them from skillet. Keep crepes covered to prevent them from drying out.

4 Spoon filling onto crepes. Sprinkle half of cheese over filling on crepes; roll up crepes. Place seam sides down in ungreased 11×7-inch (2-quart) glass baking dish. Sprinkle with remaining cheese. Bake uncovered 10 to 12 minutes or until hot.

1 Serving: Calories 260 (Calories from Fat 130); Total Fat 15g (Saturated Fat 5g); Cholesterol 90mg; Sodium 780mg; Total Carbohydrate 19g (Dietary Fiber 2g); Protein 12g

Cheesy Potato Skins

Prep Time: 26 min ▪ Start to Finish: 1 hr 40 min ▪ 8 Servings

4 large potatoes (about 2 lb)
2 tablespoons butter or margarine, melted
1 cup shredded Colby–Monterey Jack cheese blend (4 oz)
$^1/_2$ cup sour cream
8 medium green onions, sliced ($^1/_2$ cup)

1 Heat oven to 375°F. Prick potatoes with fork. Bake potatoes 1 hour to 1 hour 15 minutes or until tender. Let stand until cool enough to handle.

2 Cut potatoes lengthwise into fourths; carefully scoop out pulp, leaving $^1/_4$-inch shells. Refrigerate potato pulp for another use.

3 Set oven control to broil. Place potato shells, skin sides down, on rack in broiler pan. Brush with butter.

4 Broil with tops 4 to 5 inches from heat 8 to 10 minutes or until crisp and brown. Sprinkle cheese over potato shells. Broil about 30 seconds longer or until cheese is melted. Serve hot with sour cream and green onions.

1 Serving: Calories 120 (Calories from Fat 45); Total Fat 5g (Saturated Fat 3g); Cholesterol 15mg; Sodium 90mg; Total Carbohydrate 13g (Dietary Fiber 1g); Protein 4g

Cheese Grits

Prep Time: 20 min Start to Finish: 1 hr 10 min 8 Servings

2 cups milk
2 cups water
$1/2$ teaspoon salt
$1/4$ teaspoon pepper
1 cup uncooked white hominy quick grits
$1^1/2$ cups shredded Cheddar cheese (6 oz)
2 medium green onions, sliced (2 tablespoons)
2 large eggs, slightly beaten
1 tablespoon butter or margarine
$1/4$ teaspoon paprika

1 Heat oven to 350°F. Spray $1^1/2$-quart casserole with cooking spray.

2 In 2-quart saucepan, heat milk, water, salt and pepper to boiling. Gradually add grits, stirring constantly; reduce heat. Simmer uncovered about 5 minutes, stirring frequently, until thickened. Stir in cheese and onions.

3 Stir 1 cup of the grits mixture into eggs, then stir back into remaining grits in saucepan. Pour into casserole. Cut butter into small pieces; sprinkle over grits. Sprinkle with paprika.

4 Bake uncovered 35 to 40 minutes or until set. Let stand 10 minutes before serving.

Go for the grits! This cheesy version will make a believer out of you.

1 Serving: Calories 220 (Calories from Fat 100); Total Fat 11g (Saturated Fat 6g); Cholesterol 85mg; Sodium 340mg; Total Carbohydrate 19g (Dietary Fiber 0g); Protein 11g

6

sweet relief

Vanilla Pudding

Prep Time: 20 min ■ Start to Finish: 1 hr 20 min ■ 4 Servings

1/3 cup sugar

2 tablespoons cornstarch

1/8 teaspoon salt

2 cups milk

2 large egg yolks, slightly beaten

2 tablespoons butter or margarine, softened

2 teaspoons vanilla

1 In 2-quart saucepan, mix sugar, cornstarch and salt. Gradually stir in milk. Cook over medium heat, stirring constantly, until mixture thickens and boils. Boil and stir 1 minute.

2 Gradually stir at least half of the hot mixture into egg yolks, then stir back into hot mixture in saucepan. Boil and stir 1 minute; remove from heat. Stir in butter and vanilla.

3 Pour pudding into dessert dishes. Cover and refrigerate about 1 hour or until chilled. Store covered in refrigerator.

1 Serving: Calories 220 (Calories from Fat 100); Total Fat 11g (Saturated Fat 5g); Cholesterol 130mg; Sodium 170mg; Total Carbohydrate 26g (Dietary Fiber 0g); Protein 5g

Rice Pudding

Prep Time: 30 min ■ Start to Finish: 1 hr 30 min ■ 8 Servings

1/2 cup uncooked regular long-grain rice
1 cup water
2 large eggs or 4 large egg yolks
1/2 cup sugar
1/2 cup raisins or chopped dried apricots
2 1/2 cups milk
1 teaspoon vanilla
1/4 teaspoon salt
Ground cinnamon or nutmeg

1 In 1 1/2-quart saucepan, heat rice and water to boiling, stirring once or twice; reduce heat to low. Cover and simmer 14 minutes (do not lift cover or stir). All water should be absorbed; if not, drain excess water.

2 Heat oven to 325°F.

3 In ungreased 1 1/2-quart casserole, beat eggs with wire whisk or fork. Stir in sugar, raisins, milk, vanilla, salt and hot rice. Sprinkle with cinnamon.

4 Bake uncovered 45 minutes, stirring every 15 minutes. Top of pudding will be very wet and not set (overbaking may cause pudding to curdle).

5 Stir well; let stand 15 minutes. Enough liquid will be absorbed while standing to make pudding creamy. Serve warm, or cover and refrigerate about 3 hours or until chilled. Store covered in refrigerator.

Got leftover rice? Go ahead and use it. Put in 1 1/2 cups cooked rice, and increase the bake time by about 5 minutes.

1 Serving: Calories 180 (Calories from Fat 25); Total Fat 3g (Saturated Fat 1g); Cholesterol 60mg; Sodium 125mg; Total Carbohydrate 33g (Dietary Fiber 0g); Protein 5g

Crème Brûlée

Prep Time: 20 min ▪ Start to Finish: 7 hrs ▪ 4 Servings

6 large egg yolks	1 teaspoon vanilla
2 cups whipping cream	Boiling water
1/3 cup granulated sugar	8 teaspoons brown sugar

1 Heat oven to 350°F. In small bowl, slightly beat egg yolks with wire whisk. In large bowl, stir whipping cream, 1/3 cup granulated sugar and the vanilla until well mixed. Add egg yolks to cream mixture; beat with wire whisk until evenly colored and well blended.

2 In 13×9-inch pan, place four 6-ounce ceramic ramekins.* Pour cream mixture evenly into ramekins.

3 Carefully place pan with ramekins in oven. Pour enough boiling water into pan, being careful not to splash water into ramekins, until water covers two-thirds of the height of the ramekins.

4 Bake 30 to 40 minutes or until top is light golden brown and sides are set (centers will be jiggly).

5 Carefully transfer ramekins to wire rack, using tongs or grasping tops of ramekins with pot holder. Cool 2 hours or until room temperature. Cover tightly with plastic wrap and refrigerate until chilled, at least 4 hours but no longer than 2 days.

6 To make caramelized crust, turn on the broiler. Uncover ramekins; gently blot any condensation on custards with paper towel. Sprinkle 2 teaspoons sugar over each custard. Place ramekins in 15×10×1-inch pan or on cookie sheet with sides. Broil with tops 4 to 6 inches from heat 5 to 6 minutes or until sugar is melted and forms a glaze. Serve immediately, or refrigerate up to 8 hours before serving.

*Do not use glass custard cups or glass pie plates; they cannot withstand the heat from the broiler and may break.

1 Serving: Calories 540 (Calories from Fat 400); Total Fat 45g (Saturated Fat 25g); Cholesterol 450mg; Sodium 50mg; Total Carbohydrate 29g (Dietary Fiber 0g); Protein 7g

Oatmeal-Raisin Cookies

Prep Time: 15 min ▪ Start to Finish: 24 min ▪ About 3 Dozen

²/₃ cup granulated sugar

²/₃ cup packed brown sugar

¹/₂ cup butter or margarine, softened

¹/₂ cup shortening

1 teaspoon baking soda

1 teaspoon ground cinnamon

1 teaspoon vanilla

¹/₂ teaspoon baking powder

¹/₂ teaspoon salt

2 large eggs

3 cups quick-cooking or old-fashioned oats

1 cup all-purpose flour

1 cup raisins, chopped nuts or semisweet chocolate chips, if desired

1 Heat oven to 375°F.

2 In large bowl, beat all ingredients except oats, flour and raisins with electric mixer on medium speed, or mix with spoon. Stir in oats, flour and raisins.

3 On ungreased cookie sheet, drop dough by rounded tablespoonfuls about 2 inches apart.

4 Bake 9 to 11 minutes or until light brown. Immediately remove from cookie sheet to wire rack.

Want to save some time? Make bars. Press dough in an ungreased 13×9-inch pan. Bake 15 to 20 minutes or until light brown. Cool in pan on wire rack.

1 Cookie: Calories 120 (Calories from Fat 60); Total Fat 6g (Saturated Fat 2g); Cholesterol 20mg; Sodium 95mg; Total Carbohydrate 15g (Dietary Fiber 0g); Protein 2g

Chocolate Chip Cookies

Prep Time: 10 min ■ Start to Finish: 20 min ■ About 4 Dozen

$^3/_4$ cup granulated sugar
$^3/_4$ cup packed brown sugar
1 cup butter or margarine, softened
1 teaspoon vanilla
1 large egg
$2^1/_4$ cups all-purpose flour
1 teaspoon baking soda
$^1/_2$ teaspoon salt
1 cup coarsely chopped nuts
1 bag (12 oz) semisweet chocolate chips (2 cups)

1 Heat oven to 375°F.

2 In large bowl, beat sugars, butter, vanilla and egg with electric mixer on medium speed, or mix with spoon. Stir in flour, baking soda and salt (dough will be stiff). Stir in nuts and chocolate chips.

3 On ungreased cookie sheet, drop dough by rounded tablespoonfuls about 2 inches apart.

4 Bake 8 to 10 minutes or until light brown (centers will be soft). Cool 1 to 2 minutes; remove from cookie sheet to wire rack.

Nothing beats a chocolate chip cookie, hot from the oven. Go on—indulge!

1 Cookie: Calories 140 (Calories from Fat 70); Total Fat 8g (Saturated Fat 3.5g); Cholesterol 15mg; Sodium 80mg; Total Carbohydrate 16g (Dietary Fiber 0g); Protein 1g

Chocolate Brownies

Prep Time: 25 min ▪ Start to Finish: 3 hrs 10 min ▪ 16 Brownies

$^2/_3$ cup butter or margarine

5 oz unsweetened baking chocolate, cut into pieces

1$^3/_4$ cups sugar

2 teaspoons vanilla

3 large eggs

1 cup all-purpose flour

1 cup chopped walnuts, if desired

1 Heat oven to 350°F. Grease bottom and sides of 9-inch square pan with shortening.

2 In 1-quart saucepan, melt butter and chocolate over low heat, stirring constantly. Cool 5 minutes.

3 In medium bowl, beat sugar, vanilla and eggs with electric mixer on high speed 5 minutes. Beat in chocolate mixture on low speed, scraping bowl occasionally. Beat in flour just until blended, scraping bowl occasionally. Stir in walnuts. Spread in pan.

4 Bake 40 to 45 minutes or just until brownies begin to pull away from sides of pan. Cool completely in pan on wire rack, about 2 hours.

1 Brownie: Calories 310 (Calories from Fat 170); Total Fat 18g (Saturated Fat 8g); Cholesterol 60mg; Sodium 65mg; Total Carbohydrate 31g (Dietary Fiber 2g); Protein 4g

Molten Chocolate Cakes

Prep Time: 20 min   Start to Finish: 37 min   6 Servings

Baking cocoa
6 oz semisweet baking chocolate, chopped
1/2 cup plus 2 tablespoons butter or margarine
3 large whole eggs
3 large egg yolks
1 1/2 cups powdered sugar
1/2 cup all-purpose flour
Additional powdered sugar, if desired

1 Heat oven to 450°F. Grease bottoms and sides of six 6-ounce custard cups with shortening; dust with cocoa.

2 In 2-quart saucepan, melt chocolate and butter over low heat, stirring frequently. Cool slightly.

3 In large bowl, beat whole eggs and egg yolks with wire whisk or hand beater until well blended. Beat in 1 1/2 cups powdered sugar. Beat in melted chocolate mixture and flour. Divide batter evenly among custard cups. Place cups on cookie sheet with sides.

4 Bake 12 to 14 minutes or until sides are set and centers are still soft (tops will be puffed and cracked). Let stand 3 minutes. Run small knife or metal spatula along sides of cakes to loosen. Immediately place heatproof serving plate upside down onto each cup; turn plate and cup over and remove cup. Sprinkle with additional powdered sugar. Serve warm.

1 Serving: Calories 550 (Calories from Fat 300); Total Fat 33g (Saturated Fat 16g); Cholesterol 265mg; Sodium 170mg; Total Carbohydrate 56g (Dietary Fiber 2g); Protein 7g

Lemon Bars

Prep Time: 10 min ▪ Start to Finish: 1 hr 40 min ▪ Makes 25 Bars

1 cup all-purpose flour
$1/2$ cup butter or margarine, softened
$1/4$ cup powdered sugar
1 cup granulated sugar
2 teaspoons grated lemon peel, if desired
2 tablespoons lemon juice
$1/2$ teaspoon baking powder
$1/4$ teaspoon salt
2 eggs
Additional powdered sugar

1 Heat oven to 350°F. In small bowl, mix flour, butter and powdered sugar with spoon. Press in bottom and $1/2$ inch up sides of ungreased 8-inch or 9-inch square pan. Bake 20 minutes.

2 Meanwhile, in medium bowl, beat granulated sugar, lemon peel, lemon juice, baking powder, salt and eggs with electric mixer on high speed about 3 minutes or until light and fluffy. Carefully pour over hot crust.

3 Bake 25 to 30 minutes or until no indentation remains when touched lightly in center. Cool completely in pan on wire rack, about 1 hour. Sprinkle with powdered sugar. For bars, cut into 5 rows by 5 rows.

Love coconut? Stir in $1/2$ cup of flaked coconut in Step 2.

1 Bar: Calories 150 (Calories from Fat 60); Total Fat 7g (Saturated Fat 3g); Cholesterol 40mg; Sodium 100mg; Total Carbohydrate 21g (Dietary Fiber 0g); Protein 2g

Banana Bread

Prep Time: 15 min ▪ Start to Finish: 3 hrs 25 min ▪ 2 Loaves (24 slices each)

1¼ cups sugar
½ cup butter or margarine, softened
2 eggs
1½ cups mashed very ripe bananas (3 medium)
½ cup buttermilk
1 teaspoon vanilla
2½ cups all-purpose flour
1 teaspoon baking soda
1 teaspoon salt
1 cup chopped nuts, if desired

1 Move oven rack to low position so that tops of pans will be in center of oven. Heat oven to 350°F. Grease bottoms only of two 8×4-inch loaf pans or one 9×5-inch loaf pan with shortening or cooking spray.

2 In large bowl, stir sugar and butter until well mixed. Stir in eggs until well mixed. Stir in bananas, buttermilk and vanilla; beat with spoon until smooth. Stir in flour, baking soda and salt just until moistened. Stir in nuts. Divide batter evenly between 8-inch pans or pour into 9-inch pan.

3 Bake 8-inch loaves about 1 hour, 9-inch loaf about 1 hour 15 minutes, or until toothpick inserted in center comes out clean. Cool 10 minutes in pans on wire rack.

4 Loosen sides of loaves from pans; remove from pans to wire rack. Cool completely, about 2 hours, before slicing. Wrap tightly and store at room temperature up to 4 days, or refrigerate up to 10 days.

1 Slice: Calories 70 (Calories from Fat 20); Total Fat 2.5g (Saturated Fat 1g); Cholesterol 15mg; Sodium 95mg; Total Carbohydrate 12g (Dietary Fiber 0g); Protein 1g

Fresh Peach Cobbler

Prep Time: 31 min ▪ Start to Finish: 1 hr ▪ 6 Servings

$^1/_2$ cup sugar

1 tablespoon cornstarch

$^1/_4$ teaspoon ground cinnamon

4 cups sliced fresh peaches (6 medium)

1 teaspoon lemon juice

1 cup all-purpose flour

1 tablespoon sugar

$1^1/_2$ teaspoons baking powder

$^1/_2$ teaspoon salt

3 tablespoons firm butter or margarine

$^1/_2$ cup milk

2 tablespoons sugar, if desired

Sweetened whipped cream, if desired

1 Heat oven to 400°F.

2 In 2-quart saucepan, mix $^1/_2$ cup sugar, the cornstarch and cinnamon. Stir in peaches and lemon juice. Cook over medium-high heat 4 to 5 minutes, stirring constantly, until mixture thickens and boils. Boil and stir 1 minute. Pour into ungreased 2-quart casserole; keep peach mixture hot in oven.

3 In medium bowl, mix flour, 1 tablespoon sugar, the baking powder and salt. Cut in butter, using pastry blender (or pulling 2 table knives through ingredients in opposite directions), until mixture looks like fine crumbs. Stir in milk. Drop dough by 6 spoonfuls onto hot peach mixture. Sprinkle 2 tablespoons sugar over dough.

4 Bake 25 to 30 minutes or until topping is golden brown. Serve warm with sweetened whipped cream.

1 Serving: Calories 300 (Calories from Fat 120); Total Fat 13g (Saturated Fat 7g); Cholesterol 40mg; Sodium 240mg; Total Carbohydrate 44g (Dietary Fiber 4g); Protein 3g

Cobblers are a homey way to use fruit in season. Short on time? Try the blueberry variation—there's no peeling or pitting! Substitute 4 cups blueberries for the peaches. Omit cinnamon.

Impossibly Easy French Apple Pie

Prep Time: 25 minutes ▪ Start to Finish: 1 hr 15 minutes ▪ 6 Servings

Filling
3 cups sliced peeled apples (3 large)
1 teaspoon ground cinnamon
¼ teaspoon ground nutmeg
½ cup Original Bisquick mix
½ cup granulated sugar
½ cup milk
1 tablespoon butter or margarine, softened
2 eggs

Streusel
½ cup Original Bisquick mix
¼ cup chopped nuts
¼ cup packed brown sugar
2 tablespoons firm butter or margarine

1 Heat oven to 325°F. Grease 9-inch glass pie plate. In medium bowl, mix apples, cinnamon and nutmeg; place in pie plate.

2 In medium bowl, stir remaining filling ingredients until well blended. Pour over apple mixture in pie plate. In small bowl, mix all streusel ingredients until crumbly; sprinkle over filling.

3 Bake 40 to 45 minutes or until knife inserted in center comes out clean. Cool 5 minutes. Store in refrigerator.

1 Serving: Calories 335 (Calories from Fat 125); Total Fat 14g (Saturated Fat 3g); Cholesterol 70mg; Sodium 400mg; Total Carbohydrate 49g (Dietary Fiber 2g); Protein 5g

Chocolate Pecan Pie

Prep Time: 20 min ▪ Start to Finish: 3 hrs 40 min ▪ 8 Servings

Best Flaky Pastry
1 cup all-purpose flour
1/4 teaspoon salt
1/3 cup plus 1 tablespoon
     shortening or 1/3 cup lard
2 to 3 tablespoons cold water

Pecan Filling
2/3 cup sugar
2/3 cup butter or margarine, melted
1 cup corn syrup
2 tablespoons bourbon, if desired
1/2 teaspoon salt
3 eggs
1 cup pecan halves or broken pecans
1 bag (6 oz) semisweet chocolate chips (1 cup)

1 Heat oven to 375°F.

2 In medium bowl, mix flour and 1/4 teaspoon salt. Cut in shortening, using pastry blender or crisscrossing knives, until particles are size of small peas. Sprinkle with cold water, 1 tablespoon at a time, tossing with fork until all flour is moistened and pastry almost leaves side of bowl (1 to 2 teaspoons more water can be added if necessary).

3 Gather pastry into a ball. Shape into flattened round on lightly floured surface. Roll pastry, using floured rolling pin, into circle 2 inches larger than upside-down pie plate, 9×1¼ inches. Fold pastry into fourths; place in pie plate. Unfold and ease into plate, pressing firmly against bottom and side. Trim overhanging edge of pastry 1 inch from rim of pie plate. Fold and roll pastry under, even with plate; flute as desired.

4 In large bowl, beat sugar, butter, corn syrup, bourbon, 1/2 teaspoon salt and the eggs with hand beater. Stir in pecans and chocolate chips. Pour into pastry-lined pie plate. Cover edge with 2- to 3-inch strip of foil to prevent excess browning; remove foil during last 15 minutes of baking.

5 Bake pie 40 to 50 minutes or until set. Cool 30 minutes. Refrigerate about 2 hours until chilled.

1 Serving: Calories 630 (Calories from Fat 315); Total Fat 35g (Saturated Fat 14g, Trans Fat nc); Cholesterol 105mg; Sodium 350mg; Total Carbohydrate 76g (Dietary Fiber 3g, Sugars nc); Protein 6g

Helpful Nutrition and Cooking Information

Recommended intake for a daily diet of 2,000 calories as set by the Food and Drug Administration

Total Fat	Less than 65g
Saturated Fat	Less than 20g
Cholesterol	Less than 300mg
Sodium	Less than 2,400mg
Total Carbohydrate	300g
Dietary Fiber	25g

Calculating Nutrition Information

- The first ingredient is used wherever a choice is given (such as $1/3$ cup sour cream or plain yogurt).

- The first ingredient amount is used wherever a range is given (such as 2 to 3 teaspoons).

- The first serving number was used wherever a range is given (such as 4 to 6 servings).

- "If desired" ingredients and recipe variations were not included (such as sprinkle with brown sugar, if desired).

- Only the amount of a marinade or frying oil that is absorbed by the food during preparation was calculated.

Ingredients Used in Recipe Testing and Nutrition Calculations

- The following ingredients, based on most commonly purchased ingredients, are used unless indicated otherwise:

- large eggs, 2% milk, 80%-lean ground beef, canned chicken broth and vegetable oil spread containing at least 65% fat when margarine is used.

- Solid vegetable shortening (not butter, margarine, or nonstick cooking spray) is used to grease pans.

Equipment Used in Recipe Testing

- Cookware and bakeware without nonstick coatings were used, unless otherwise indicated.

- No dark-colored, black or insulated bakeware was used.

- When a pan is specified, a metal pan was used; a baking dish or pie plate means ovenproof glass was used.

- An electric hand mixer was used for mixing when mixer speeds are specified.

Metric Conversion Guide

VOLUME

U.S. Units	Canadian Metric	Australian Metric
¹/₄ teaspoon	1 mL	1 ml
¹/₂ teaspoon	2 mL	2 ml
1 teaspoon	5 mL	5 ml
1 tablespoon	15 mL	20 ml
¹/₄ cup	50 mL	60 ml
¹/₃ cup	75 mL	80 ml
¹/₂ cup	125 mL	125 ml
²/₃ cup	150 mL	170 ml
³/₄ cup	175 mL	190 ml
1 cup	250 mL	250 ml
1 quart	1 liter	1 liter
1 ¹/₂ quarts	1.5 liters	1.5 liters
2 quarts	2 liters	2 liters
2 ¹/₂ quarts	2.5 liters	2.5 liters
3 quarts	3 liters	3 liters
4 quarts	4 liters	4 liters

WEIGHT

U.S. Units	Canadian Metric	Australian Metric
1 ounce	30 grams	30 grams
2 ounces	55 grams	60 grams
3 ounces	85 grams	90 grams
4 ounces (¹/₄ pound)	115 grams	125 grams
8 ounces (¹/₂ pound)	225 grams	225 grams
16 ounces (1 pound)	455 grams	500 grams
1 pound	455 grams	¹/₂ kilogram

MEASUREMENTS

Inches	Centimeters
1	2.5
2	5.0
3	7.5
4	10.0
5	12.5
6	15.0
7	17.5
8	20.5
9	23.0
10	25.5
11	28.0
12	30.5
13	33.0

TEMPERATURES

Fahrenheit	Celsius
32°	0°
212°	100°
250°	120°
275°	140°
300°	150°
325°	160°
350°	180°
375°	190°
400°	200°
425°	220°
450°	230°
475°	240°
500°	260°

NOTE: The recipes in this cookbook have not been developed or tested using metric measures. When converting recipes to metric, some variations in quality may be noted.

Index

*Whatever's on the menu,
make it easy with Betty Crocker*

**Betty Crocker
chicken
tonight**

100 Recipes for the Way You Really Cook

**Betty Crocker
comfort
food**

100 Recipes for the Way You Really Cook

**Betty Crocker
party
food**

100 Recipes for the Way You Really Cook

**Betty Crocker
quick
fixes**

100 Recipes for the Way You Really Cook